# Footprints on the Banks of Sycamore Creek

John R. Coles and Carolyn Adcock-Smith

ISBN-10: 1545482268
ISBN-13: 978-1545482261

# DEDICATION

Betty Adcock Darnell

We would like to dedicate this book to Betty Adcock Darnell. We express our appreciation and affection for Betty who provided photographs, old letters, vivid memories, and hours of pure joy to our efforts on this book.

## Acknowledgments

We gratefully acknowledge the following people who helped us put this book together.

Yolanda Reid, Robertson County Archives, Barbara Jewell, Cornelia Masters, Molly E. Frey, Lois Barnes Binkley, and our many cousins who shared photographs and memories.

We also thank BJ Smith for being patient and helpful while Carolyn took so much time doing the research for the book. BJ also went with her to the cemeteries, to the archives, and on her quest to find where something was. He was her driver, photographer and supporter.

# Contents

# Introduction

In the late 1600s and early 1700s, there were so many people named Adcock in the Virginia Colony, I'm surprised they didn't just name it the Adcock Colony. It may be impossible to trace the family line back to this early period. Ship passenger lists show early Adcock arrivals in Virginia included Toby Adcock who arrived in 1672, Thomas and Jane Adcock in 1687, and Simon Adcock in 1702. There is a John Adcock who was born in Virginia in 1691. Adcock families were in every part of Virginia, but those who are likely our direct ancestors lived in Buckingham County, around Willis Creek, before the American Revolution.

By that time, there were many Johns, Josephs, Williams, Henrys and Toms. All of these Adcocks seemed intent on naming their children in honor of their mothers, fathers and aunts and uncles, so that it becomes impossible to know which John or Henry or Joseph is a father or brother in our family line. There are many historical records that include births, marriages and deaths of Adcocks in early Virginia. The problem is that the connections between them and the Adcocks now living around Sycamore Creek in Tennessee, are missing. Record keeping in those days was sporadic. When records were kept, they were sometimes lost to floods and fires. What is left is a piece of fabric with many broken threads.

We can draw some notion of those early Adcocks from the facts we know. They were farmers. They looked after each other. They raised large families, and they stuck together. These qualities are repeated, generation after generation. This can be seen in the historical records from the earliest Adcock family members who left Virginia and settled along the north and south forks of Sycamore Creek, to their descendants who, over two hundred years later, still live along its banks or in the nearby hills and hollers.

In 1770, in the County of Spotsylvania, in the Colony of Virginia, members of the local Baptist Church had been so mistreated by followers of the Church of England that they felt it necessary to move.

In the book, "Towards a History of the Baptists in the Provinces of Maryland, Virginia, North Carolina, South Carolina, Georgia" by Morgan Edwards, completed in 1772, we find a description of their new church.

"Buckingham [is] so called from the county where the meeting house is 170 miles WNW from Williamsburg, and 240 SSW from Philadelphia. The place of worship is 20 feet by 20 feet built in 1772 on land given by Seth Cason."

"The families [number] about 200 whereof 68 persons are baptized and in communion. The minister [is] Rev Rene Chastain."

"They organized from Lower Spotsylvania whereof they had been a branch till they were constituted into a district church, May 1772. The constituents were, Rene Chastain and wife, Joseph Carter and wife, Robert Huddleston and wife, William Anderson and wife, Seth Cason and wife, Wm Johnston, Wm Hammonds, John Epperson, George Epperson, Thos Holland, Steph Garret, John Acres and wife, Henry Baher, James Ford, Philip Vert, Benj Briston, Benj Gots, Wm Peasley, John Arnold, Hanna Hudgins, Ann Carter, Sarah Wheeler, Lettice Hammond, Sara Guthery, Elis Sharoon, Eliz Gols."

When we read the list of names associated with the Buckingham Baptist Church, and compare them with other historical records, we see that the Adcock family in Buckingham was closely associated with this group.

On November 17, 1785, Thomas Paslay married Winney Adcock. On February 13, 1787, John Adcock married Sally Wheeler. Surety for the marriage bond was posted by Thomas Pasley. The marriage was performed by Rev. Rene Chastain. This is from historical records, "Marriages of Buckingham County, Virginia" in the possession of the Virginia Historical Society. Another marriage performed by Rev. Rene Chastain was between Nathaniel Frances and Eleanah Adcock on November 11, 1786.

Other historical records show names that are commonly found among the Adcock family members who settled along Sycamore Creek. According to the records of the Court held for Buckingham County on December 9, 1782, Anderson Adcock and Joseph Adcock were paid for wintering beef. Land records in Buckingham County between May 1784 and June 1785, include transactions of Anderson Adcock and George Adcock.

An even earlier record, a tax list from 1764, found in the records of Prince Edward County, shows taxes paid by some residents of Buckingham County. These include Joseph Adcock, who appears to have owned 400 acres and three slaves named Edmund, Jack and Genne; Anderson Adcock, who owned 100 acres; John Adcock, who owned 200 acres and a slave named Flora; Henry Adcock, who owned no land or slaves; and another Joseph Adcock, who owned 200 acres and a slave named Lucey.

From Buckingham County tax records for 1773 and 1774, at the Virginia State Archives in Richmond, we find Anderson Adcock, George Adcock, two men named John Adcock, and three named Joseph Adcock.

In a mutilated old account book kept by John Epperson at his tobacco warehouse and general store on the Appomattox River in Buckingham County at a settlement called Planterstown, we find Joseph Adcock listed with others.

These historical records are given to show the reason so many believe the Adcock family in Robertson and Davidson Counties in Tennessee, descended from the Adcock families of Buckingham County, Virginia. We know that John A. Adcock, who settled on Sycamore Creek in 1822, was born and grew up in Buckingham County, Virginia. We know that Carter Adcock was born in Virginia and migrated to Tennessee at an early age. That migration story would have been typical of the early pioneers.

Family tradition holds that we are descended from John A. Adcock of Virginia. There are many who say that John A. Adcock, who was a soldier in the American Revolution, was Carter Adcock's father. Others say he was Carter's grandfather. We have exhausted the available historical records without finding credible evidence to support either claim. We found contradictions in the historical records, so we acknowledge that we will likely never know for sure.

John A. Adcock, resident of Robertson County, must not be confused with John Adcock, resident of Davidson County. John A. Adcock applied for a pension as a Revolutionary soldier in Robertson County in 1834. John Adcock, of Davidson County, applied for a pension in 1819, in Smith County. John A. Adcock arrived in Robertson County in 1822. He came after Carter Adcock, who arrived before 1817.

There is a monument to John A. Adcock in the Adcock Cemetery (Anderson Adcock Cemetery) at Ridgetop. The marker was placed there in recent years by the Sons of the American Revolution (SAR). There are probably unmarked graves in the Adcock Cemetery (Anderson Adcock Cemetery), but, there is no historical evidence to justify the claim that John A. Adcock is buried there. The fifty-two acre property on which the cemetery is located was purchased by John A. Adcock in 1844. Anderson Adcock acquired it on August 18, 1855.

The historical marker says that John A. Adcock died in 1837. Even the date of his death is not certain. Pension records indicate John A. Adcock was still receiving payments as late as September, 1848. It is possible that payments were made after his death, but not likely for over ten years after he died.

In records of the March Term, 1847, Robertson County Court[1], it is written, "A paper writing purported to be the last will and testament of John A Adcock deceased was produced in open Court for probate and there upon came I R Reeder Subscribing witness to said paper writing who being first sworn depose and say that he were acquainted with John Adcock the Testator and in his life time and that he acknowledged in his presence to be his last will and Testament and that he was at that time in his proper mind and that he attested said paper writing at his request."

This would actually support the idea that John A. Adcock could be buried in the Adcock Cemetery (Anderson Adcock Cemetery) at Ridgetop, because he died around the time the land was purchased by Anderson Adcock. This would also support the idea that John A. Adcock is a member of our family line. Unfortunately, we have no concrete evidence to support either idea. While we do know John A. Adcock's Will was filed in Robertson County Court, the Will has not been found. We also know, from court records, that John A. Adcock left everything he owned to his daughter, Winney Adcock.

---

[1] Robertson County Tennessee Archives, County Court Minute Book 12, Pages 397-398

Perhaps, someday, it will be found and give us evidence linking him to our family tree. For now, his link to our family line is just family tradition.

We want to include information on the land owned by John A. Adcock because it is land that has an important place in the running history of the Adcock family along the banks of Sycamore Creek. There was a parcel of land amounting to 100 acres, surveyed on July 4, 1829, by Roland Wingo and Elijah McGraw, for John A. Adcock. This survey is recorded on page 181, Land Surveys, Robertson County Archives. The entry reads:

> "State of Tennessee, Robertson County, by virtue of Entry No. 627, dated February 2, 1828, I have surveyed for John A. Adcock one hundred acres of land in said county on the dividing ridge between the north and south prongs of Sycamore Creek. Beginning on two red oaks on the south side of a hill running north crossing Rules branch in all eighty poles to a small Spanish oak on the point of a ridge thence east ninety-four poles to a black gum in the west boundary line of Carter Adcock one hundred acres survey thence south with his line crossing a branch in all fourteen poles to a white oak his southwest corner of said tract thence east with his line one hundred and twenty eight poles to a black gum and dogwood on the point of a ridge thence south sixty six poles to a Chestnut and Spanish oak on the point of a ridge thence west crossing two branches in all two hundred and twenty two poles to the beginning."

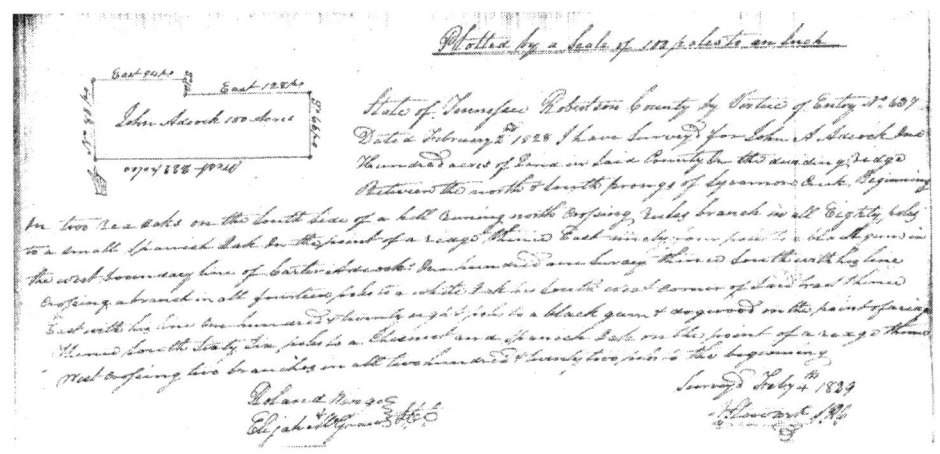

Survey for John A. Adcock, dated July 4, 1829

The Land Grant, 10052, corresponding to the survey, was recorded on April 11, 1831.

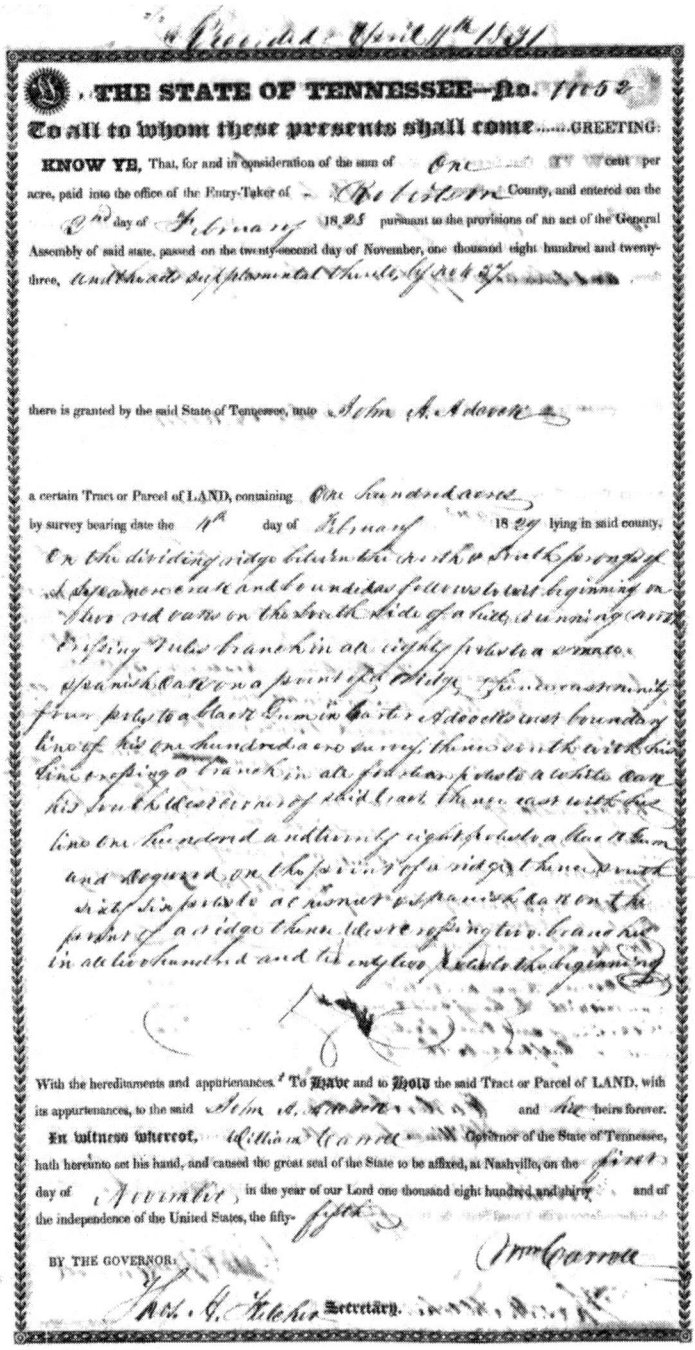

John A. Adcock acquired another fifty-two acres in 1844. This is the beginning of the Adcock family ownership of the land on which the Adcock Family Cemetery (Anderson Adcock Cemetery) on Walker Road is located. This land was surveyed on November 17, 1839. The survey reads:

"State of Tennessee, Robertson County. November 28th 1839 – I have surveyed for John A. Adcock fifty two acres of land on Rules branch and bounded as follows Beginning at three red oaks the corner of the tract of land on which he now lives – thence north 62 poles to an ash thence west 52 poles to an Ironwood on a branch thence with its meanders in all 114 poles to a beach on the bank of said branch thence south 20 poles to a white oak – Tate's corner thence east with his line 156 poles to his corner an oak and beach thence to the beginning. Surveyed November 17th 1839 by W. S. Perry."

State of Tennessee } By Virtue of Entry No 1129 dated
Robertson County } November 28th 1839 – I have surveyed
for John A. Adcock fifty two Acres of land on
Rules branch and bounded as follows Begining
at three red oaks the corner of the tract of land on
which he now lives thence north 62 poles to an ash
thence west 52 poles to an Ironwood on a branch thence
with its Meanders in all 114 poles to a beach on the
bank of said branch thence south 20 poles to a white
oak ~~thence~~ Tates corner thence east with his line 156
poles to his corner an oak and beach thence to the
begining –

Surveyed November 17th 1839
By W S. Perry [illegible]

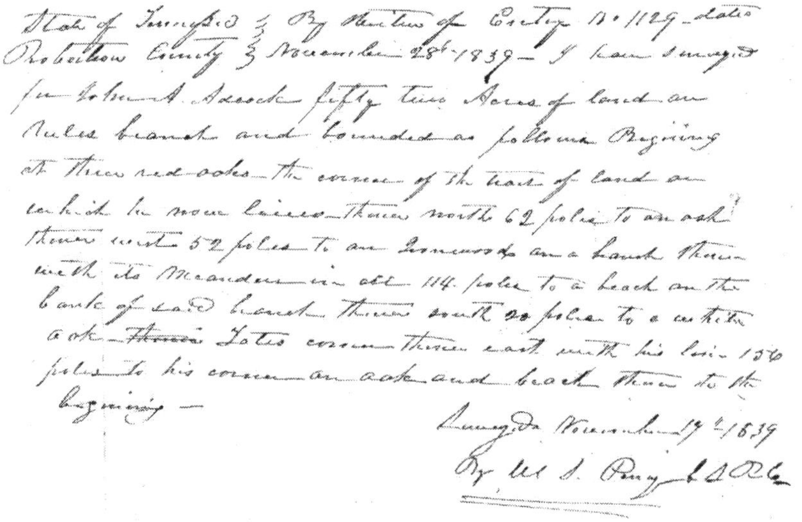

The Land Grant, Number 17746, was made on July 19, 1844.

What follows is a story based on the historical facts available to us. We hope it will help you understand the hardships and uncertainties our ancestors endured. We believe this will give you a sense of their hopes and expectations. It is a story of promise and peril, common to all who were the American pioneers. The Adcock families who settled along Sycamore Creek arrived between 1800 and 1815. We can confidently trace our family line back to Carter Adcock and Adelia Railey.

# Chapter One

## Carter Adcock Married Adelia Railey

### (1817 to 1837)

Carter Adcock was born about 1801, in Virginia, probably in Buckingham County. Sometime before 1817, he came to Tennessee. The earliest document we have found that we can directly connect to Carter is his marriage record. He married "Dilly" Railey on October 9, 1817 in Sumner County, Tennessee. They did not live in Sumner County, but applied for their license there.

In those days, when a couple obtained a marriage license, the groom had to promise to pay a penalty if the couple did not marry. This bond was typically posted by the groom and someone who knew and trusted him. In the case of Carter and Adelia, the bond was signed by Isaac Peairs.

Marriage Bond of Carter Adcock and Adelia Railey. She was known as "Dilly"

It is interesting that the infamous "Bell Witch" was first observed on the Bell farm in Robertson County in 1817, the year Carter and Adelia married. Stories of that unearthly spirit were told and retold from generation to generation. Stories of goblins and witches have been popular entertainments in the Adcock households from early times to the present day, as you will read later in our story.

The next document related to Carter Adcock is found in the Minutes of the Robertson County Court, 1818-1826. On page 57, is written, "May, 1818 – Ordered by the court that Moses Paisley survey the road from the top of the ridge to Bailey's pond and that with the following hands keep said road in repair according to law, to wit, Carter Adcock, James Baines, Joseph Stanley, Nobel Warren, Zachariah Warren, Moses Stanley, Henry Adcock and Joshua Brumbalow."

It seems that the state took claim to the road and ordered the people who lived along it to keep it in good repair. There were entries in these Minutes that mention the road again in 1824, 1825, and 1826. Each time, Carter Adcock is mentioned, along with others, and is ordered to keep the road "in repair according to law."

Carter Adcock could get into trouble. In November, 1818, he was brought to court on an "Indictment for a Riot." It is not clear what the riot was about, or how big it was. But, a jury was called and Carter was found "guilty in manner and form as charged" and fined one dollar. We can only imagine what Adelia thought about that.

There are irregularities in the early Federal Census records regarding the children of Carter and Adelia Adcock. Anyone who has tried to follow their family tree by using these early Federal Census records knows that they can only be used as a general guide. They were not compiled on pre-printed forms. They were hand drawn with a quill pen. Only the name of the head of the household was recorded. All others were unnamed and marked as male or female of an age range. To make it more unreliable, the unnamed people may or may not be related to the head of the household.

We have made every effort to compare the census records to other sources, such as tombstone inscriptions, death certificates, marriage records and court documents when they were available. Starting with the Federal Census of 1850, each member of the household was named and their age was given. With that cautionary statement, we will move our story along.

In 1820, Carter was living in Robertson County. For those who know where the old house was located, this seems wrong, but it is right. Carter built another house on the Davidson County side of Sycamore Creek after 1845. The line separating Robertson and Davidson Counties ran through Carter's farm. Over the years the county line moved around between the North Fork and South Fork of Sycamore Creek.

Living near Carter and Adelia were William Carter and Moses Pasley and their families. These are names we also found in documents from Buckingham County, Virginia. On the same page of the 1820

Federal Census, where we find Carter Adcock, we also find Henry Adcock with his family.

This census indicates that Carter and Adelia had two children, a boy and a girl. The age of the boy, between 10 and 15 years-of-age, is certainly wrong. Carter would have been only nine or ten-years-old, when the boy was born. The census taker may have marked the wrong box. Of course, this child may also have belonged to someone else, or a mistaken mark on the part of the census taker. The girl is their daughter, Nancy Adcock. Nancy was born in 1819 or early 1820.

Carter's and Adelia's son, Anderson Adcock, was born on November 10, 1820. At that time, there were only twenty-three states in the Union. Carter and his family focused on the demanding challenges of everyday life on the farm. Clearing land, planting crops, tending livestock and countless other jobs were backbreaking tasks that required constant attention from all available hands, including other family members and neighbors.

Robert Taylor Adcock was born on February 1, 1822. Franklin Adcock was born about 1828. Andrew Jackson, who had run unsuccessfully in 1824, ran again in 1828, and prevailed. He was elected the nation's seventh President, and the first from Tennessee.

In the February Term 1828, John Adcock and Carter Adcock appeared in court on Peace Warrants. Apparently, they had engaged in a fight with some other men and were arrested. They were both released, but John Adcock was ordered to pay court costs.

Carter Adcock had to be making plans for his growing family. With a wife and four children, Carter chose to expand his farm by taking advantage of an Act of The Tennessee State General Assembly passed in 1823, that encouraged development of unimproved lands.

The lands around Sycamore Creek had belonged to Native American tribes of Creek and Cherokee and factions known as the Chickamauga, Chickasaw and Choctaw. It was part of a large tract of land purchased from the Cherokee in 1777, by Richard Henderson of the Transylvania Land Company. It was part of North Carolina until 1789, when it was ceded to the federal government. Tennessee achieved statehood in 1796, but, North Carolina reserved the right to satisfy land claims it had made to Revolutionary soldiers. Because North Carolina held the land records, it was almost ten years later before the state of Tennessee could offer land grants.

This is an area of rolling hills covered in thick forests of oak and hickory. There are areas of bluestem prairie called barrens. The soil is rich. There are ample streams and plenty of fish and game. The land around Sycamore Creek has fertile fields and high bluffs that drop off suddenly into beautiful bottom lands and creeks.

There are two land grants listed for Carter Adcock in "Tennessee Land Grants, Volume 1." Each grant is for one hundred acres.[2]

On January 26, 1828, Carter Adcock paid the "Entry Taker" in Robertson County for the opportunity to acquire 100 acres of land on Sycamore Creek. The land was surveyed on February 2, 1829, by A. Steward. Abner Adcock and Carter Adcock are listed on the survey with "SCC" beside their names. This meant they were "Sworn Chain Carriers." Family members helped the surveyor and had to take an oath that they would be honest. The purchase was recorded on April 11, 1831. Carter paid one cent per acre.

Survey of one hundred acres of land dated February 2, 1829.

---

[2] "Tennessee Land Grants, Volume 1, Book 12, page 373, Grant Number 10038, and page 386, Grant Number 10051."

The description reads:

"Beginning on a white oak near James McIntosh's east boundary line of a sixty acre survey in the name of McIntosh and Cheatham turns east one hundred and twenty six and a half poles to two Dogwoods and a Hickory, thence south one hundred and twenty six and one half poles to a poplar and white oak in the head of a hollow, thence west crossing a branch in all one hundred and twenty six and a half poles to a hickory and hornbeam on the point of a ridge, thence north crossing a branch in all one hundred and twenty six and a half poles to the Beginning."

Recorded April 11th 1831

## THE STATE OF TENNESSEE--No. 10038

### To all to whom these presents shall come........GREETING:

**KNOW YE,** That, for and in consideration of the sum of *One* cent per acre, paid into the office of the Entry-Taker of *Robertson* County, and entered on the 26th day of *January* 18 68 pursuant to the provisions of an act of the General Assembly of said state, passed on the twenty-second day of November, one thousand eight hundred and twenty-three, *and the acts supplemental thereto of which*

there is granted by the said State of Tennessee, unto *Carter Adcock*

a certain Tract or Parcel of LAND, containing *one hundred acres* by survey bearing date the *2nd* day of *February* 18 29 lying in said county, *on the ridge between the north and south forks of Sycamore creek, and bounded as follows to wit: Beginning on a white oak near James McIntosh's east boundary line of a half acre survey in the name of McIntosh & Chatham runs east one hundred and twenty six and a half poles to two Dogwoods & a Hickory, thence south three hundred and twenty six north 40 poles to a poplar & white oak in the head of a hollow, thence west crossing a branch in all one hundred and twenty six and a half poles to a hickory and hornbeam on the point of a ridge, thence north crossing a branch in all one hundred and twenty six and a half poles to the Beginning*

With the hereditaments and appurtenances. To **Have** and to **Hold** the said Tract or Parcel of LAND, with its appurtenances, to the said *Carter Adcock* and *his* heirs forever. **In witness whereof,** *William Carroll* Governor of the State of Tennessee, hath hereunto set his hand, and caused the great seal of the State to be affixed, at Nashville, on the *first* day of *November* in the year of our Lord one thousand eight hundred and thirty, and of the independence of the United States, the fifty-*fifth*

BY THE GOVERNOR.

*Wm Carroll*

*Thos H Fletcher* Secretary.

The Land Grant, Number 10038, resulting from the survey of February 2, 1829

6

We know that this Land Grant was for 100 acres located in Robertson County "on the ridge between the north and south forks of Sycamore Creek." The Grant is "by the said State of Tennessee, unto Carter Adcock," and "for and in consideration of the sum of one cent per acre paid into the office of the Entry Taker of Robertson County and entered on the 26th of January, 1828. This Land Grant was recorded on April 11, 1831.

For anyone interested in the process of surveying land in the 1820s, it was done by men using a Surveyor's Chain, which is 66 inches long. These were literally chains made up of 100 links. Four "poles" equal one chain. They found a starting point and pulled the chain directly toward a second point. They anchored the end of this chain in the ground and pulled the other end toward the second point. They repeated this until the chain reached the second point. They repeated this process until they had measured all sides. The tools were primitive by today's standards, but the results were amazingly accurate.

We know that some of the land purchased by members of the Adcock family was "School Land." Simply put, the State of Tennessee set aside some of the land it held for the benefit of public education. It began in 1806, when the United States Congress passed an act "to authorize the State of Tennessee to issue grants and perfect title to certain lands therein described, and to settle the claims to the vacant and unappropriated lands within the same." One condition was certain lands should be set aside for schools and colleges. In 1823, the State of Tennessee passed an act that provided that "the proceeds from the sale of and from state taxes on certain vacant lands north and east of the Congressional Reservation line" should go into the school fund. In 1825, the sale of School Land was authorized. Much of that land sold for as little as 12 ½ cents an acre. It is difficult to know which land was actually "School Land." But, in early tax records, it was taxed at a different rate. For a detailed explanation of "School Lands," we recommend "Tennessee Public School Lands" by Virginia Williams, published in volume 3, number 4, of the 1944 *Tennessee Historical Quarterly*.

Another one hundred acres was surveyed for Carter Adcock on February 2, 1829. This survey lists Isaac Reeder and Abner Adcock as Sworn Chain Carriers. This describes the land as located on the north fork of Sycamore Creek. "Beginning on a white oak in Daniel Buie's South boundary line of his middle fifty acre Survey on said creek, runs with his line East passing his corner of said tract and with the line of his other fifty acre tract crossing two branches in all one hundred and seventy nine poles to an ironwood. Thence South crossing a branch in all eighty nine and one half poles to a Dogwood on the side of a hill, thence West crossing a branch in all one hundred and seventy nine poles to a small hickory on the east boundary line of a three hundred and fifty acre Survey of the said Daniel Buie's, thence North with his line eighty nine and one half poles to the beginning." This survey was also registered by A. Stewart.

East 179.60.

Carter Adcock
100 acres

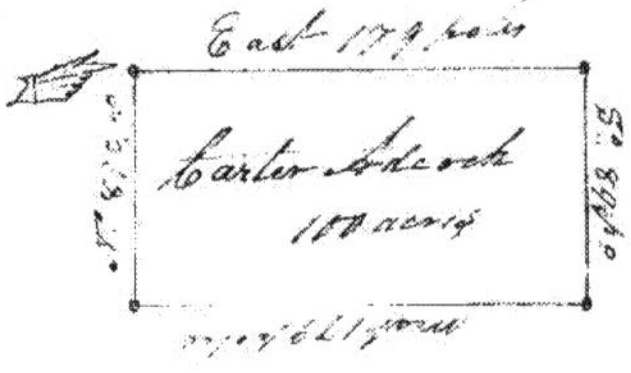

State of Tennessee Robertson County, By Virtue of Entry No. 436 Dated January 6th 1826 I have Surveyed for Carter Adcock One Hundred acres of Land in Said County on the north fork of Sycamore Creek, Beginning on a white Oak in Daniel Buies South boundary line of his middle fifty acre Survey on Said Creek, Runs with his line East passing his Corner of Said tract & with the line of his other fifty acre tract Crossing two branches in all One hundred & twenty nine poles to a____ Thence South Crossing a branch in all eighty nine & one half poles to a Dogwood on the Side of a hill thence West Crossing a branch in all One hundred & Seventy nine poles to a small Hickory in the east boundary line of a three hundred & fifty acre Survey of the Said Daniel Buies Thence North with his line eighty nine & one half poles to the Beginning

Isaac Reader
Abner Adcock

Surveyd Feby 2d 1829
A Stewart D.S.

Recorded April 11th 1831          389.

# THE STATE OF TENNESSEE—No. 10051

## To all to whom these presents shall come......GREETING:

**KNOW YE,** That, for and in consideration of the sum of *One* _____ cent per acre, paid into the office of the Entry-Taker of *Robertson* _____ County, and entered on the *5th* day of *January* 18*26* pursuant to the provisions of an act of the General Assembly of said state, passed on the twenty-second day of November, one thousand eight hundred and twenty-three, *and the acts supplemental thereto by No 436*

there is granted by the said State of Tennessee, unto *Carter Adcock*

a certain Tract or Parcel of LAND, containing *One hundred acres* by survey bearing date the *2nd* day of *February* 18*29* lying in said county, *On the north fork of Sycamore creek and bounded as follows, to wit: Beginning on a white oak on Daniel Buis Tenth branch, his line of his middle branch very on said creek running with his line east passing his corner of the said 500 acre tract, and running with the line of his upper 500 acre tract crossing two branches in all one hundred and ninety three poles to an ironwood, thence South crossing a branch in all eighty nine poles to a Degard on ... a hickory side thence west crossing a branch in all one hundred and twenty nine poles to a small hickory in the east boundary line of said Daniel Buis 330 acres survey thence north with said line eighty nine poles to the Beginning*

With the hereditaments and appurtenances. To **Have** and to **Hold** the said Tract or Parcel of LAND, with its appurtenances, to the said *Carter Adcock* _____ and *his* heirs forever. **In witness whereof,** *William Carroll* _____ Governor of the State of Tennessee, hath hereunto set his hand, and caused the great seal of the State to be affixed, at Nashville, on the *first* day of *November* in the year of our Lord one thousand eight hundred and thirty and of the independence of the United States the fifty- *fifth*

BY THE GOVERNOR:

*Wm Carroll*

*Thos. H. Fletcher* Secretary.

The Land Grant, Number 10051, resulting from the survey of February 2, 1829

9

This was an active period for Carter. In addition to records of land purchases, we found that he managed to get into more trouble for fighting. On Wednesday, November 11, 1829, Morris Railey was ordered to court on a charge of assault and battery. He failed to appear. Carter Adcock was also named and failed to appear. The court ordered a penalty of fifty dollars, which was their bond amount.

The home of Carter and Adelia Adcock on Sycamore Creek was filling up during the 1830s. Cynthia Adcock was born on March 18, 1834. Albert Adcock was born around 1835. John C. Adcock was born on January 27, 1836. Will Adcock was born around 1836. Their daughter, Martha Adcock was born around 1837.

It was about this time that Nancy, Carter's and Adelia's oldest daughter, married John Anderson. She was about eighteen years old. When she and John married, Carter Adcock gave them a bed valued at twenty-five dollars. Their son, Carter Lee Anderson, was born on May 10, 1836.

In 1837, Carter and Adelia celebrated their 20th wedding anniversary. A lot had happened in their lives since they married. They now had nine children. Carter owned at least two hundred acres of land along Sycamore Creek. This included land that was cleared for farming and wooded land for hunting and fishing.

# Chapter Two

# The Family Grows

The home of Carter and Adelia Adcock was crowded with nine children. The children shared bedrooms. Some shared beds. Some helped in the house, cooking, preparing food to store for the winter, spinning and sewing. Others helped outside the house, planting, hunting, storing meats in the smokehouse, and chopping wood for the fire. For some of us in what is now the "older generation," this sounds quite familiar. For the Adcock families in the early 1950s, before electricity was run from the highway back the old dirt road to Sycamore Creek, life hadn't changed much in a hundred years. Kerosene lamps had replaced candles, flour and meal could be purchased at the store, but not much else was different.

For Carter's family, in the 1830s, church was not a regular activity. There were few ministers to preach. Families and neighbors gathered from time to time for prayers and baptisms in the creek. Revivals and camp meetings were sometimes held by the Baptists and Methodists. These occasions provided an opportunity to worship. They also offered a chance to discuss crops, exchange news and gossip, and conduct business.

Entertainment, in those days, was family and friends singing and playing music together. Whether it was one guitar and a few people on the porch, or a band at a barn dance filled with friends and neighbors, the only music they had was what they made for themselves. There were not a lot of opportunities to socialize. There were no schools in the area. This meant that the children of Carter and Adelia did not have the opportunity or the time to learn to read or write.

Elizabeth Adcock was born on December 22, 1838. Carter Adcock appears on the District 22, Davidson County tax roll of 1839. Other men on this list were John A. Adcock, Abner Adcock, Asa Adcock, John Adcock, Silas Adcock, Henry Adcock, and Beverly Adcock. From other sources we know that most of these men, like Carter, came from Buckingham County, Virginia. On October 22, 1840, Carter and Adelia had a son. They named him Morris Riley Adcock.

We don't know what happened to Nancy's husband, John Anderson. On November 5, 1845, Nancy married Luther Barnes.

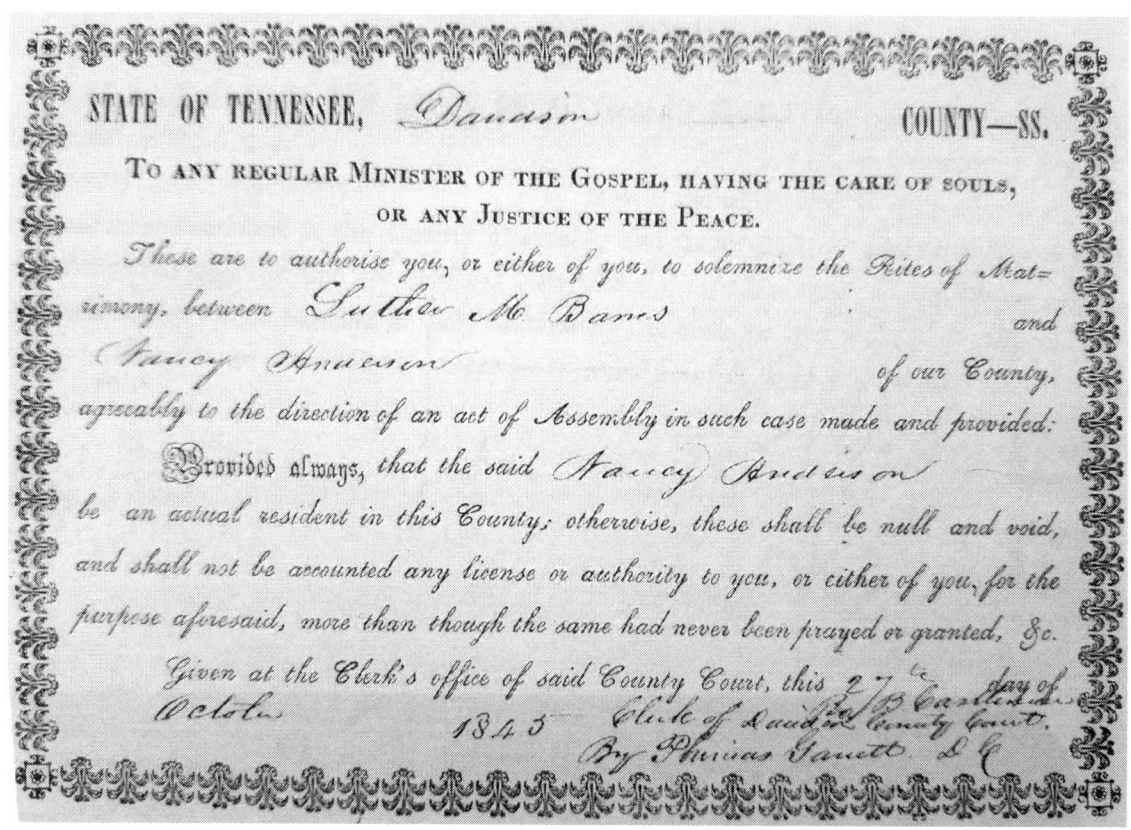

Marriage License of Nancy Adcock Anderson and Luther M. Barnes

Her father gave them one cow and calf valued at twenty-five dollars. They began building a family. By 1850, they had two children; Robert N. Barnes, born September 26, 1848, and Sarah "Dillie" Barnes, born in August, 1849. Carter L. Barnes, formerly Carter Lee Anderson, was living with his mother, Nancy, and step-father, Luther Barnes. He was fourteen years old. Luther Barnes, who was born in North Carolina in 1822, was a blacksmith.

In an Index to deeds in Davidson County (1784-1871) there is a record of the transfer of 174 acres on Sycamore Creek from William H. Bedford to Carter Adcock. The transfer is listed as being in Volume 7, page 262, and dated January 30, 1845. The record is hand-written and difficult to read. The basic facts are that Carter Adcock purchased the 174 acres for "the sum of three hundred and forty-four dollars." It was described as "a certain tract of land lying in the Counties of Davidson and Robertson on both sides of Sycamore Creek."

Mary Frances Adcock was born to Carter and Adelia on March 14, 1848. Carter's and Adelia's oldest son, Anderson, married Caroline Smiley on June 14, 1849. Caroline Smiley was born October 29, 1831. She was the daughter of Samuel Smiley and Hessie Warren. On his marriage to Caroline Smiley, Carter Adcock gave to his son, Anderson, one horse valued at one hundred dollars, one bed valued at twenty five dollars.

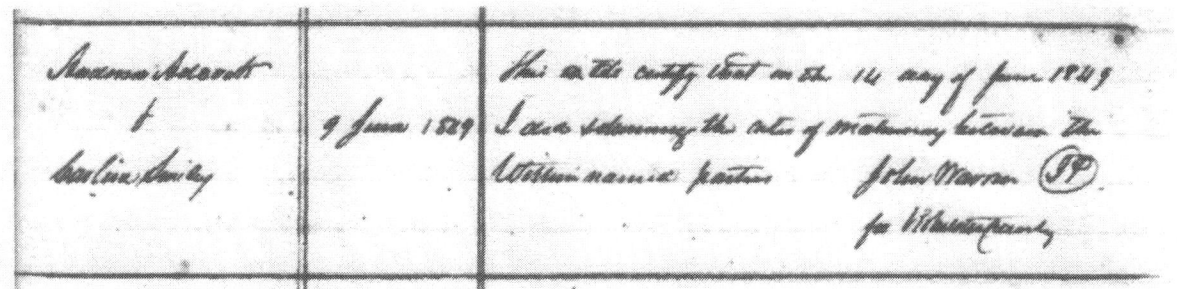

Marriage record of Anderson Adcock and Caroline Smiley

The Agricultural census for 1850, tells us a great deal about Carter's farm. According to that report, Carter had forty acres of "improved" land and two-hundred acres of "unimproved" land, valued at $800. He had four horses, one mule, and three milk cows. He had one hundred pigs. He raised three hundred bushels of "Indian" corn.

Indian corn was not as sweet as the hybridized corn we know today. It was used for milling into cornmeal, for feeding farm animals, and as fertilizer for crops. It was also cooked and eaten, but, by today's standards, it would taste pretty bland.

The 1850 Federal census was the first to name each person living in a household. Carter and Adelia had eleven children living at home. They were Robert, Franklin, Will, Cynthia, Albert, John, Martha, Elizabeth, Mary, Riley, and Collins, who was six months old. Collins Adcock was born on April 22, 1850.

It was about this time that Carter Adcock built a two-story log house on Sycamore Creek. We are fortunate to have Annie Biggs Adcock's stories. In the one that follows, she recalls the old house and a funny story to go with it.

My husband and I planned to go fishing one evening. We lived just below a well-known hole of water called the Blue Hole. Just the other side of this hole of water there was an old log house two stories high. The old log house had been hand built by my husband's grandparents about ten years before the Civil War. They had spent their days in the old log house and died. The old house was vacant. We were sitting on the big rock of the Blue Hole fishing, when all at once we heard a terrible noise at the old house. It sounded like something running up and down the steps. My husband said he was going over there and see what all that noise was. So, he did. We had heard all kinds of tales about what was going on around this old house. Well, he tried to slip up and see if he could find out something and he did.

I had one brother and he had been up the creek for something. He lived close to us and he was going home when he also heard the noise and stopped. He went in this old house and there was a bunch of goats that had got inside and, somehow, got the door shut. They were running up and down those steps. My brother was chasing them just to hear the racket. We all laughed and went home.

The 1850 Federal Census for Robertson County, District 12, shows Anderson Adcock living with his wife, Caroline, and daughter, Artemissa, known as Missy. Anderson, age thirty, was a farmer. Caroline was age eighteen. Their daughter, Missy, was one-month old. They are listed next to Anderson's sister, Nancy, and her husband Luther Barnes.

John A. Adcock's Last Will was presented in Robertson County Court during the March Term in 1847. His daughter, Winney, was the Executrix of his estate. On October 12, 1849, a suit was filed against Winney Adcock, Executrix, by David Darden, Surviving partner of Darden and Kelly. In Circuit Court Book C, page 547, the following statement can be found:

> "State of Tennessee, Robertson County. I command you to summon Winney Adcock, Executris of John A. Adcock, deceased, to appear before me on the 4th day of October, 1849, to show cause if any she has why Execution should not be issued against her as Executrix of John A. Adcock, deceased, staying on a Judgement that Darden and Kelly obtained against FD Tait and Jo Bouie and John A. Adcock stayed in the same before A Justice in favor of Darden and Kelly on the 13th day of June, 1846, for the sum of $15.65 and the cost and interest this the 23rd day of August, 1849."

According to the U.S. Federal Census Mortality Schedule of 1850, Winneford "Winney" Adcock, who was born in Virginia, died in Robertson County, District 12, in May, 1850, of unknown causes. She had been ill for seven months. That would mean she became ill at exactly the time the lawsuit was filed against her by David Darden.

We do not know the reason for the debt owed Darden and Kelly, but it forced the sale of the land Winney Adcock inherited from her father.

In Robertson County Deed Book 9, pages 96 and 97, we learn how the land owned by John A. Adcock and inherited by his daughter, Winney, came into the hands of Anderson Adcock, son of Carter Adcock. It is a long passage, so we will only quote the relevant part.

> "Alf Pike, Sheriff, to David Porter, 18th August, 1855. Whereas David Porter recovered a Judgement against Winney Adcock for the sum of ( ) debt, and cost of suit in the Circuit Court of Robertson County, Tennessee at September Term, 1849, upon Venditioni Exponas issued from said Term, which came to the hands of R W Murphey, Sheriff of Robertson County, and after giving the lawful notice on the ( ) day of ( ) 1849, at the Court House door in Springfield, sold a certain lot of land lying and being in the County of Robertson and

District No. 12, on Rules Branch of Sycamore Creek, number of acres ninety and a half, adjoining the lands of Asy Adcock, McGraw and others, sold as the property of said Winney Adcock to satisfy the above named Venditioni Exponas and David Porter being the highest and last bidder. Therefore the same was struck off to him for the sum of twenty seven dollars."

This shows that the land belonging to Winney Adcock was sold to David Porter at Springfield, on August 18, 1855. On the same page we find that David Porter sold that same parcel of land to Anderson Adcock, on the same day.

"David Porter to Anderson Adcock, 18th August, 1855. I David Porter have this day bargained and sold, and do hereby transfer and convey to Anderson Adcock his heirs and assigns forever, for the consideration of one hundred dollars to me paid, a tract of land containing by estimation ninety and a half acres, be the same more or less, lying on the waters of Rules Branch of Sycamore Creek in the 12th Civil District of Robertson County, Tennessee, and bounded as follows, to wit, Beginning at a stake and pointers, formerly three red oaks, on the South side of a ridge thence north 80 poles crossing Rules branch to a heap of rocks and pointers, thence east 94 poles to a sower wood, thence south 14 poles to a dead white oak Asa Adcock's corner east 100 poles to a gum and dogwood thence south 66 poles to a Chestnut and Spanish oak on a ridge thence N 89 ¼ W 200 poles to the Beginning."

The description of this land compares in most respects to the lands surveyed for John A. Adcock in 1829 and 1839. The court records show the progressive transfer of this land from John A. Adcock, to his daughter, Winney Adcock, to David Porter, to Anderson Adcock.

From the 1850 Federal Census, taken on December 9, 1850, we learn that Polly A. Railey, age seventeen, was living with her parents, Morris and Mary Railey. Ten days later, on December 19, 1850, Robert Adcock and Polly A. Railey were married.

Marriage license of Robert Adcock and Polly Ann Railey

In 1860, Nancy and Luther Barnes were living in Davidson County. They had two additional children. Catherine, who was born February 18, 1854, was called Catie. John Frank Barnes was born November 8, 1854. Nancy's son by John Anderson lived with them. He was twenty-two years old. He is listed as Lee Barus (Barnes).

For those observant readers who noticed the Barnes family was living in Robertson County in 1850, but in Davidson County in 1860, do not think they moved. They were living in the same house. The county line separating Robertson County and Davidson County was redrawn in 1860.

According to "History of Davidson County, Tennessee with Illustrations and Biographical Sketches of its Prominent Men and Pioneers" by Prof. W. W. Clayton, published in 1880, "The boundary-line established in 1859 begins at a point on Sycamore Creek a little above John C. Puckett's, and runs down that creek and with the Robertson county-line to a point between Asa Adcock and Wilkerson's old burnt steam-mill." This book states, "July 2, 1860, a portion of Robertson County was annexed to this district [in Davidson County]."

By 1860, Carter had fifty acres of "improved" land and one hundred and fifty acres of "unimproved" land. He now had three horses, six mules, and three milk cows. He had thirteen sheep and fifty pigs. The value of his livestock was estimated to be $1,600. That would be over $43,000 in 2017 dollars. He raised seven hundred bushels of corn and produced fifty pounds of wool from his sheep.

Cater Adcock's farm: U.S. Selected Federal Census Non-Population Schedule of 1860.

Carter cleared fifty acres of land between 1850 and 1860. In one of her stories, Annie Biggs Adcock described the process of clearing unimproved land. She was born in 1892, so the process she describes would be the same process that Carter used.

> When I was a small girl at home with my parents, people raised mostly what we ate. So, we didn't have enough cleared land. Most of this land was loaded with big heavy timber, trees over three feet through in diameter. These trees had to be got out of the way so the land would be cleared. This was called 'new ground.'

> So, the men all worked together. They would have a big log rolling. Few people living now ever saw one. I saw several when I was small. We had a hill called Billy Goat Hill covered in big white oaks and black oaks. My father threw a big log rolling. About twenty-five neighbor men came with hand spikes. That meant a big dinner had to be cooked. It took several neighbor women to help. They would kill several chickens, made dumplins, had some old fashioned pies cooked, plenty of coffee and milk.

> The men would cut these big trees and saw them up with what they called cross-cut saws.

Hadn't thought of a chain-saw. They would take these hand spikes and drive them into the end of the logs and split them. I have often thought of how much money they would have brought if we only had them now. But, they was set fire to and burned-up so as to clear the ground. It was not waste then, because there was no sale for them. On the new ground, we grew tobacco and other things. Then it was a pasture. It grew up in wild blackberry vines. We picked all we could use. And people all around came and picked.

People living in the Carter Adcock household in 1860, according to the census, included Carter, Delia, Will, Albert, John, Martha, Elizabeth, Riley, Mary, Collins, and Ellen, who was five months of age. Ellen was the infant daughter of Carter's and Adelia's son, Anderson Adcock, and his wife Caroline.

Anderson and Caroline Adcock added four children between 1850 and 1860. Hessie Ann Adcock was born in 1852. Martha Jane Adcock was born in 1854. Sylvanus Benton Adcock, who was called "Sill," was born in 1857. Their daughter, Everline, was born in 1859.

Robert and Polly had three children during this period. Malandy was born in 1855, Carter Edward was born on January 1, 1856, and John Franklin Adcock was born on March 28, 1858.

Cynthia Adcock married Currenton J. "C.J." Williams in Davidson County, on July 20, 1854.

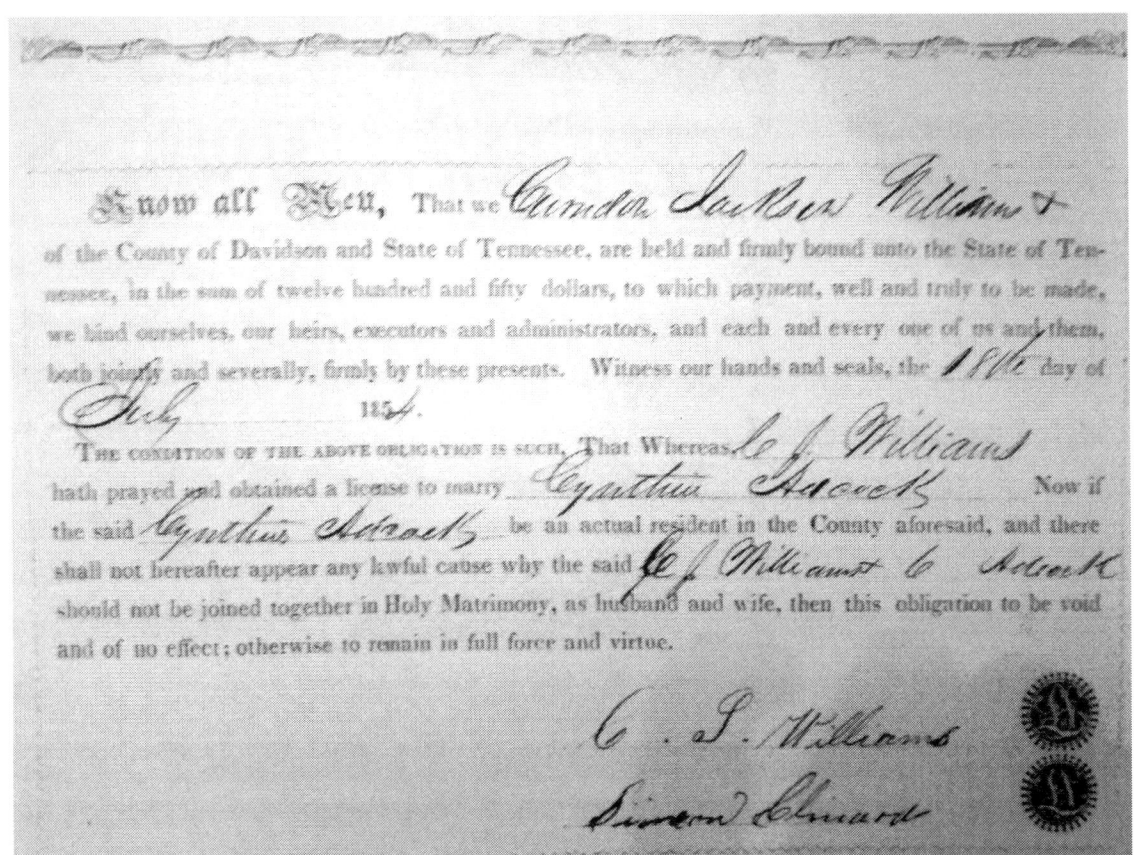

Marriage license of Cynthia Adcock and C.J. Williams

C.J. Williams was born in January, 1831, in Nashville. Their son, James Williams, was born in June, 1860. On November 17, 1861, their daughter, Elizabeth, was born. By this time, the American Civil War had begun. One might think that the family was isolated from the turbulence and tragedies of this historic conflict. They would be wrong.

# Chapter Three

## The Adcock Family During the Civil War

### (April 12, 1861 – May 10, 1865)

Before we continue the story of our Adcock family, we need to give this brief description of the conditions created by the Civil War in the area where they lived. Tensions between the northern and southern states grew over many years. By 1860, it was clear that the nation was divided and the southern states would secede from the Union. In February, 1861, Tennessee had voted to stay in the Federal Union. When Fort Sumter, in Charleston, South Carolina, was fired on by Confederate troops on April 12, 1861, President Lincoln called on each state to send troops south to put down the rebellion. On June 8, 1861, Tennessee reversed its position and voted to secede from the Union.

Tennessee seceded from the Union on June 8, 1861

Brigadier General Ulysses S. Grant's forces captured Fort Henry, on the Tennessee River, on February 6, 1862. He quickly moved east and captured Fort Donelson, on the Cumberland River, ten days later. These were major victories for the north and gave the Union forces easy access for their advance across Tennessee.

It was a Sunday morning in February, 1862. By ten o'clock, rumors that Fort Donelson had surrendered reached the streets of Nashville. People were told that 35,000 Yankee soldiers were in Clarksville, and would arrive in Nashville by three o'clock in the afternoon. Confusion and terror spread quickly. Church services were dismissed early. People began fleeing by carriages and trains. Many were afraid the Yankees would burn Nashville to the ground. Those who stayed spent an uneasy night.

Monday morning came but no Yankees were to be seen. The Post Office closed and moved to Murfreesboro. The newspapers stopped publishing. Stores closed down. For ten days a melancholy gloom hung over the city. To protect the city from advancing troops, the railroad bridge was burned and the cables of the suspension bridge connecting Nashville with Edgefield, now East Nashville, were cut.

On Sunday, February 23rd, Mayor Cheatham was told that members of the Ohio cavalry company had arrived in Edgefield. He took a boat across the river to meet with them. They assured him they would do their best to protect the rights and property of the citizens of Nashville. On Tuesday, February 25th, a gunboat and several other ships were seen on the Cumberland River, approaching Nashville.

A good description of the event was printed in the 1867 Nashville City Directory. "Curiosity was on tiptoe, and hundreds hastened to the Lower Landing to see the monster, for a gunboat was a greater curiosity than an elephant, as well as witness the debarkation of the Federal troops. The fleet continued to approach nearer the city, and then opposite the Gas-works, the gunboat was made fast to the opposite shore. The 'Diana' steamed up to the Landing with the Sixth Regiment of Ohio Volunteers, the United States flag flying, and the band playing 'Hail Columbia.' A few, among them were some who had professed devotion to the Southern Confederacy, greeted the 'invaders' with a few huzzahs."

In a proclamation from Mayor Cheatham, he assured the public safety and protection. He requested that "business be resumed, and all our citizens, of every trade and profession, pursue their regular vocations." The proclamation also outlawed the sale of liquor. Mayor Cheatham called upon the people of the surrounding country to resume their commerce with the city and bring in their market supplies, especially wood, butter and eggs, assuring them they would be "fully protected and amply remunerated."

Although Robertson County was occupied territory and no major battles were fought within its borders, some military action did take place there. The L&N Pike, roughly where U.S. 41 is now, along the eastern border of the county was often used by both armies to move men and materials. As was often the case, these armies foraged off the land as they traveled.

In a story published in the Robertson County Times in 1910, one local resident recalled the troops who crossed the area, saying, "… those who remained overspread the neighborhood, hungry and all-devouring as the locust of the Egyptian plague." Thousands of men moved along the highways and railroads during the war. They devoured huge amounts of food. They intimidated local residents, hoping to break their fighting spirit. They sometimes burned the houses and barns of the rebels.

Federal troops would occupy Nashville for the remainder of the war. Springfield was also occupied by Federal troops. The Adcock families on Sycamore Creek found themselves living between two cities occupied by Union forces. For the entire four years of the war, they must have lived in constant fear. The events of the war would have been topics of daily discussion.

At this time, Carter's and Adelia's daughter, Elizabeth Adcock, was involved with a young man who worked in Nashville. Elizabeth, who was called "Bettie," was living with her parents on Sycamore Creek. She was about twenty-three years old. The man Bettie was interested in was James Cooper. When war broke out, Bettie was certainly seeing James. They were married less than seven months after Nashville was occupied by Federal troops.

Marriage license of Elizabeth Adcock and James Cooper

It was about this time that Carter's and Adelia's son, Albert, met the young woman who would become his wife. She was living in the same household with Elizabeth's beau, James Cooper. We don't know how Bettie Adcock came to know James Cooper. But, we do know quite a lot about the Cooper family and how they came to live in Nashville.

James Cooper was born on Christmas Day in New York, in 1836. Before 1850, his family moved to Jamestown, in Fentress County, Tennessee. They lived down the road from John and Elizabeth Oakes. John Oakes was a blacksmith and farmer. Their daughter, Martitia Oakes and her daughter, Rosanna, lived with them. Rosanna's father is unknown. In 1854, The Oakes family moved to Benton, Arkansas, leaving behind, one son, Rama Oakes, and little Rosy Oakes, who was seven years old.

Henry A. Cooper, James' older brother, had been in Nashville since 1853. He advertised that he was a manufacturer of tin, copper and sheet iron ware, and a dealer in cooking and heating stoves.

Others in the Cooper family joined Henry in Nashville in 1857. They brought Rosanna Oakes with them. Little Rosy Oakes was about ten years old. We don't know why the Cooper family brought her to Nashville.

In 1860, the Coopers were living in a large house at 81 South Cherry Street. Cherry Street is now 4<sup>th</sup> Avenue. It was a full house. James Cooper lived with his parents and three brothers. Rosy Oakes lived there, too. She was thirteen.

James and Charles Cooper were tinners. A tinner is a person who makes things out of tin. They were also called tinkers and tinsmiths. In the 1800s, many common objects such as milk pails, plates, bowls, pitchers, and other objects were made of tin. Tin didn't rust.

James Cooper and Bettie Adcock were married on September 7, 1862. Bettie and James Cooper's first child, William E. Cooper, was born in 1863. Their daughter, Mary Margaret Cooper, was born in 1865. It must have been through Bettie that her older brother, Albert Adcock, met Rosy Oakes. Albert and Rosy were married on March 22, 1865. Their daughter, Madora Adcock, was born later that year.

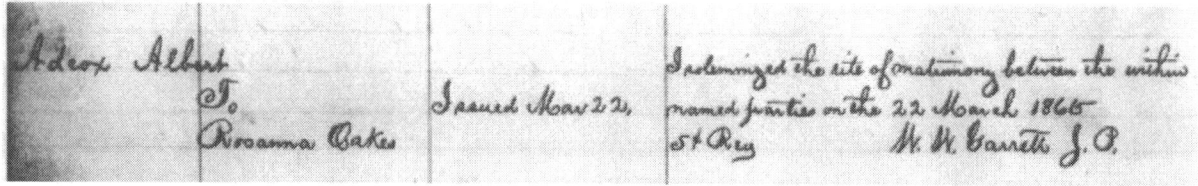

Marriage record of Albert Adcock and Rosanna Oaks

Carter Adcock gave to Elizabeth Adcock at her marriage to James Cooper, a bed valued at twenty-five dollars, and a cow and calf, valued at twenty-five dollars. He gave the same to his son, Albert, at his marriage to Rosy Oakes. Bettie and James moved to the area around Sycamore Creek after they married. Albert and Rosy did the same.

Throughout the war, Union troops continually took food, forage, wagons, and animals from the people of Robertson County and Davidson County, usually without payment. The Confederate cavalry was also in the area. One such group was John Hunt Morgan and his Raiders. His men destroyed parts of the Edgefield and Kentucky railroad in an effort to slow the movement of Union troops. They burned the railroad trestle at Ridgetop, less than ten miles from Carter Adcock's house on Sycamore Creek.

Another threat to rural farmers during the Civil War was from renegade groups of soldiers on both sides, who stole whatever they could find from the isolated families. Fear of these bandits led the farmers to hide their valuables such as silverware and money. There are many stories of fruit jars full of gold coins buried near the farmers' homes or boxes of silverware and jewelry hidden in caves in the bluffs above Sycamore Creek.

For all of the Adcock families, daily life was tinged with fear. They would have kept their guns loaded and within easy reach. Hunting would have been a dangerous activity. One might encounter military troops, or worse, a band of renegades or bush whackers.

Anderson Adcock, and his wife, Caroline, had two daughters, Mary Ellen and Caroline "Callie," during the war. Mary Ellen Adcock was born on November 18, 1861. Callie Adcock was born on May 21, 1864. Robert Taylor Adcock and his wife, Polly, had two children born during the war, Cordelia Ann Adcock, born on June 22, 1861, and Mary Ida Adcock, born on May 12, 1864.

Carter's and Adelia's daughter, Martha Matilda Adcock, gave birth to a girl named Laura Linda Adcock, on March 5, 1862. There is no documentation showing who her father was.

Carter and Adelia must have worried about their daughter, Cynthia, whose husband, C.J. Williams, enlisted on January 28, 1862. This would have left Cynthia to take care of their infant daughter, Elizabeth. C.J. was discharged in June, 1865.

Mary Frances Adcock married David Smiley around 1864. David Smiley was the son of Samuel Smiley and Hessie Warren. David was a brother to Caroline Smiley, who married Anderson Adcock, and Mary Frances Smiley, who married Morris Riley Adcock. Mary's father, Carter, gave them one bed valued at twenty five dollars one cow and calf valued at twenty five dollars.

All of the people living around Sycamore Creek would have talked about the hundreds of local men who were away fighting in the war. These were people they knew. They would have heard, from time to time, that someone's father or brother would never come home.

The history books are full of horrible stories of death and destruction suffered by the soldiers on both sides. Unfortunately, those books are also full of stories about the terrible things that happened to innocent civilians, like the Adcock families, living for four long years in the grip of war.

# Chapter Four

# Life after the Civil War

When the war finally ended, in May, 1865, people felt a mixture of relief, foreboding, and sadness. No one knew how the changes would affect them. The endless months of fighting were over, but many friends and neighbors had died. Reconstruction and the war's aftermath continued for several more years.

One of Annie Biggs Adcock's stories tells of the uneasy period immediately following the Civil War.

> My husband's father, Morris Riley Adcock, told me he remembered seeing wounded men walking the ridge road going home from the Civil War. After the war, gangs of rough men, some local deserters, decided to make life easier by stealing and robbing anyone in the community. They rode horses and mules up to a place and took anything of value and rode away. Grandpa Adcock said he saw them coming and ran home and warned his daddy, Carter Adcock.

> The men in the family with the exception of one, sick with fever, took all the food and meat to a cave across the creek above the Blue Hole. It was a high place on a ledge. They could shoot them if they came near the cave. But, they rode to the house. The women offered no resistance, so they pilfered the house, even taking the feather bed from under the sick brother, and leaving him lying on the floor. After they were gone, the men returned the food and valuables from the cave.

After the war, life on the Adcock farms slowly returned to its normal routine. Martha Adcock married John W. Hatfield on January 3, 1866. Carter Adcock gave them a wedding gift of one bed valued at twenty five dollars, one cow and calf valued at twenty five dollars. John W. Hatfield was a Wheelright. This meant he made and repaired wooden wheels. He is a bit of a mystery. The 1870 census states he was born in Tennessee, and his parents were of foreign birth. The 1880 census states he, and his parents, were born in France.

Marriage License of John Hatfield and Martha Adcock, issued January 2, 1866

Tyler Adcock was born to Anderson and Caroline Adcock on January 17, 1867. Robert Taylor Adcock and his wife, Polly, had their daughter, Lemmie, in 1867. Albert and Rosy Adcock had little Edward on March 13, 1867.

Morris Riley Adcock married Mary Francis Smiley on April 11, 1867. Mary Frances was the daughter of Samuel Smiley and Hessie Warren. She was a sister to Caroline Smiley who married Riley's brother, Anderson Adcock. Annie Biggs Adcock recalled Mary Smiley Adcock.

> Mary Smiley Adcock, my husband's mother, was a fine housekeeper. She spun thread on a spinning wheel and made all their socks. They had sheep and they sheared the wool and washed it, carded it and made little rolls about a half a foot long out of the wool and spun it into thread on the spinning wheel. I had never heard one before and it scared me half crazy. I ran home and got my mamma and we went to see what it was. We came to where she was spinning on the porch. I thought it was a terrible sight.

> She quilted three or four new quilts every fall. They didn't can much. But, there was no end to drying apples and sliced pumpkins. They killed hogs and saved every one of the entrails to make soap. They also raised geese which they picked to make feather beds and pillows. The creek bottoms were full of geese.

Franklin Adcock married Nancy Jane Wilson in Cheatham County, Tennessee, on August 30, 1866.

Marriage record of Franklin Adcock and Nancy Jane Wilson

Jane was sixteen. Franklin, at forty-two, was older than Jane's father. There is an odd thing about that marriage. The Justice of the Peace who married Franklin and Jane, was Joseph Heriges. In 1899, Franklin married Joseph Heriges' daughter, Mary Jane Heriges. But, that's getting ahead of our story.

Nancy Jane Wilson was born on June 6, 1850, in Murray County, Georgia, the daughter of Edward Wilson and Elizabeth Burlinson Wilson.

Carter Adcock gave to his son, Franklin Adcock, at his marriage with Jane Wilson, one mule valued at fifty dollars one bed valued at twenty five dollars.

How Franklin Adcock met Jane Wilson is unknown. The Wilson family lived in Georgia during that time. Jane's sister, Rebecca Wilson, married Andrew Jackson Knight in Cheatham County, Tennessee, in 1867.

Carter and Adelia Adcock celebrated their 50th Wedding Anniversary in 1867. At that time, they had thirteen children and at least thirty grandchildren. Three of their sons, William, John, and Collins were still living with them. The family was not focused entirely on their farms. They were also involved in the civic lives in their community.

Printed in the "Republican Banner" of Nashville, dated December 24, 1867, is a list of citizens chosen to work as "Judges and Clerks" in the Davidson County special election for Judge of the Criminal Court to be held on January 4, 1868. The election "Judges for District 24 were Albert Adcock, Carter Adcock, and John Adcock." The "Clerks" were Joseph J. Garrett and Luther Barnes. The notice states that, "The official will observe the following rules in the performance of their duties, viz:

1. The Judges will open the polls in accordance with the law, (nine o'clock a.m.) at the usual places in their respective wards and districts.
2. Certificates of registration printed on colored paper have been invariably issued to white voters, those issued to colored voters are of a lighter hue; the attention of the Judges is particularly called to this fact.

3. A duplicated copy of the returns in each ward and district will be delivered to the Commissioner of Registration.

A similar notice appeared in the "Republican Banner" on October 23, 1868, "for the election of Electors for President and Vice President, one for each Congressional District and two for the State at large; also for a member of the Forty-first Congress for the Fifth Congressional District." The election was held on November 3, 1868. The election "Judges for District 24 were Albert Adcock, Carter Adcock, and John Adcock. The "Clerks" were Joseph J. Garrett and Luther Barnes.

This was the time Forest Grove Methodist Church began. From "Greenville Methodist Church History" we find some information on the history of Forest Grove Methodist Church.

> Forest Grove Methodist Church is located in Davidson County four miles north of Joelton, Tenn., on the Springfield Highway. It is one of the four churches on the Joelton Circuit. Having been built around the year 1870, it is one of the old landmarks in the county. Exact dates are hard to obtain as no records were kept.

There was a one-room log house on the cemetery land that was used as a school and a church when a preacher could be obtained. It is unclear whether this was built as the church, or a proper church building was later built.

Sometime in late 1869 or early 1870, Albert Adcock died. Two days later, Albert's wife, Rosy, died. Their son, Edward "Ed" Adcock was taken in by Anderson and Caroline Adcock. Their daughter, Madora, was taken in by Carter and Adelia Adcock.

Morris Riley Adcock was the administrator of Albert's estate. The settlement of that estate was made on December 28, 1871 and recorded on May 10, 1872. This settlement shows that Morris Riley Adcock found $150 in gold and silver and $234.50 in cash in Albert's house. He collected $655.55 in sales and another $313 in outstanding notes due Albert at the time of his death.

An Inventory and Account of Sale, recorded on May 6, 1872, shows each item owned by Albert Adcock, and who purchased those items. Albert's father, Carter Adcock, bought a rifle for $2.00.

Albert's brothers bought several items. Morris Riley bought a set of horse harnesses, a chopping axe, an iron wedge, a cedar churn, and a looking glass for a total of $18.70. Robert bought a cow and calf for $25.25. Collins, bought a navy pistol for $5.50. John bought a scythe and cradle for $1.50, and William bought an oven, lid, hooks, frying pan and shovel for $1.15. Anderson bought ten barrels of corn for $50.50. Franklin bought the remainder of Albert's corn for $3.10. C.J. Williams, Albert's brother-in-law, bought ten hogs for $24.50. Others, many of them Albert's neighbors, bought the remainder of his belongings.

Morris Riley paid Albert's and Rosy's medical expenses, which amounted to $72.25. He paid his brother, Anderson, $254 for the care of Albert's and Rosy's two children. He paid $7 in fees connected with the settlement. The balance of Albert's estate amounted to $1,016.80.

Settlement of Albert Adcock's Estate recorded on December 28, 1871

On Friday morning, February 23, 1872, at the courthouse in Nashville, Franklin Adcock was appointed to be the Guardian of Ed and Madora, the minor orphan children of Albert and Rosy Adcock. He gave a bond in the amount of $2,500 with Carter Adcock and I.R. Reeder as his securities. On March 2, 1872, Franklin received the balance of Albert's estate, which was $1,016.80. This money was to be held by him for Ed and Madora until they were of legal age.

Madora was seven years old. She was living with her grandparents, Carter and Adelia. Ed was five years old and living with his uncle and aunt, Anderson and Caroline Adcock and their nine children.

Anderson and Caroline had their hands full with a farm and eleven children. Anderson had 15 acres of "improved" land. This was the land he was farming. He owned 100 acres of woodland. He had one horse, one mule and two milk cows. He had eleven sheep and fifteen pigs. He raised 100 bushels of Indian corn and 35 bushels of oats. In such a household, there is always room for one more. Taylor Adcock was born in February, 1873.

On March 21, 1872, Nancy's and Luther's son, Robert, married Martha Melinda Adcock in Robertson County. Melinda Adcock was the daughter of Nancy's brother, Robert Taylor Adcock and his wife, Polly.

At this time, Robert Taylor Adcock was living in District 12, Robertson County. Living with Robert and his wife, Polly, were sons, Carter E. Adcock, and John Franklin Adcock, and daughters Cordelia Ann, born in 1861, Mary Ida, born in 1864, and Laminzer "Lemmie", born in 1867, and son, Robert Henderson "Hen" Adcock, born in 1869. Gip Taylor Adcock, son of Robert and Polly, was born on July 28, 1872.

Franklin Adcock was living with his wife, Jane, and their children, Annie and Media. They lived near Franklin's brother, Riley, and his wife, Mary Adcock. Down the road was the home of Carter and Adelia Adcock.

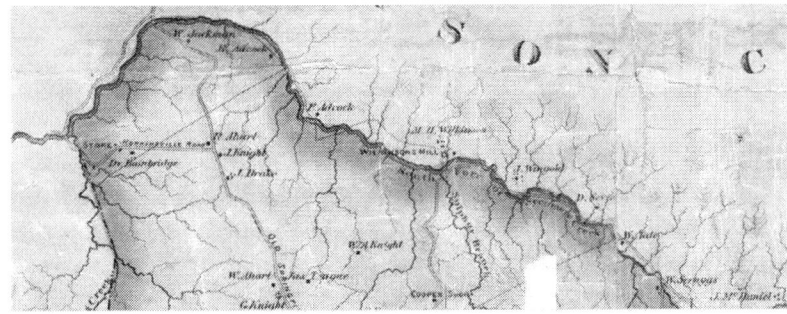

1871 Map of norther part of Davidson County. The line weaves back and forth along the South Fork of Sycamore Creek. On the map can be found the homes of Riley Adcock and Franklin Adcock. The location of Wilkinson's Mill is also shown.

Cynthia and C.J. Williams were living in Nashville. C.J. is listed as a rag dealer. This should have provided enough to live on. The rag trade flourished after the Civil War. According to the book, "Cash for Trash: Recycling in America" the rag business was second only to scrap iron after the war. "In 1866, the price of cotton and linen rags more than quadrupled due to the scarcity caused by the war. The domestic supply could not keep up with demand from the paper mills…"

Possibly motivated by the death of his son, Albert, Carter Adcock wrote his will in 1874. Following is the text of his will.

In the Name of God Amen.

I Carter Adcock, of Davidson County State of Tennessee, being of Sound mind and memory and considering the uncertainty of this transitory state of existence, do , therefore, make, ordain, publish and declare this to be my Last Will and Testament.

That is to Say,

Item 1$^{st}$ After all my lawful debts have been paid and discharged, the remainder, or residue of my estate both personal and real, I dispose of as follows.

Item 2$^{nd}$ I will to my beloved wife Dillie Adcock my farm including the Dwelling house and all that appertains to the same, together with all the Lands I may be in possession of at my death, with all the household and kitchen furniture for her support during her natural life.

Item 3$^{rd}$ I have given off to my oldest children who have married as follows to wit, I gave to my daughter Nancy at her first marriage with John Anderson one bead valued at twenty five dollars, and at her second marriage with Luther Barnes, one cow and calf valued at twenty five dollars. I gave to my son Anderson Adcock one horse valued at one hundred dollars, one bead valued at twenty five dollars, the said horse and bead was given to my said son, at his marriage with Caroline Smiley. I gave to my son Robert Adcock at his marriage with Pollie Ann Railey, one horse valued at one hundred dollars, one bead valued at twenty five dollars. I gave to my son Franklin Adcock at his marriage with Jane Wilson one mule valued at fifty dollars one bead valued at twenty five dollars. I gave to my son Albert Adcock at his marriage with Rosy Oaks one bead valued at twenty five dollars, one cow and calf valued at twenty five dollars. I gave to my daughter Cyntha at her marriage with Currenton Williams one bead valued at twenty five dollars one cow and calf valued at twenty five dollars. I gave to my daughter Martha at her marriage to John Hatfield one bed valued at twenty five dollars, one cow and calf valued at twenty five dollars. I gave to my daughter Elisabeth at her marriage with James Cooper one bead valued at twenty five dollars, one cow and calf valued at twenty five dollars. I gave to my daughter Mary at her marriage with David Smiley one bead valued at twenty five dollars one cow and calf valued at twenty five dollars. I gave to my son Riley Adcock at his marriage with Mary F. Smiley one cow and calf valued at twenty five dollars. I have not given him bead or a horse, but it is my desire and will that he may be made equal with any other children. It will be observed that my sons Franklin and Albert Adcock before mentioned has not gotten as the other boys at their marriages, and also that my daughters Nancy, Cyntha, Elisabeth, Martha and Mary at their marriages have not gotten as much as my sons. It is my will that they all be made equal.

Item 4$^{th}$ My three sons William, John, and Collins Adcock are still living with me and are a great help to me in the decline of life, but I have not given them anything. It is my will that each one of the said sons last mentioned be made equal with my other children mentioned above.

Item 5th  It is my will that if all of the three sons now living with me, Inlc William, John, and Collins above mentioned shall stay with me and my afflicted wife and help us and assist in taking care of us in our decline of life, disease or disability, that each son or in case that two or only one does so, that as they or he may make a reasonable charge for his kindnesses and extra service.

Item 6th  It is my will that Laura Linda Adcock daughter of my daughter Martha Hatfield be made equally and have as much of my estate, at my death or the death of my said wife, as my other children mentioned above.

I appoint my son Franklin Adcock Executor to this will.

This 5th day of March, 1874

Carter (his X mark) Adcock

We the undersigned do hereby testify that we have written our names as Subscribing witnesses to the above document at the request and desire of the said Carter Adcock and who acknowledge the same to be his act and deed.

This 5th day of March, 1874

R.G. Glover of Cooper Town, Robertson County Tennessee

I.R. Reeder

Note: The word "bead" appears several times in Carter's will. It is a spelling variation of "bed" that was common in wills of the late 19th century. Cater gave each child a bed, cow and calf, when each got married. Those were very practical and traditional gifts for a newly married couple at that time.

Family portrait from around 1874 showing, seated left to right, Caroline Smiley Adcock (wife of Anderson Adcock), Anderson Adcock, Carter Adcock, and Adelia Adcock.
The children are unidentified[3]

On February 16, 1877, Carter's wife, Adelia, died. Carter died nine months later on November 16, 1877. They had been married for sixty years. They raised thirteen of their own children, and a few of their grandchildren. Their deaths were a major tragedy for the family and closed a chapter in the family's history.

---

Headstone of Carter Adcock in the Carter Adcock Cemetery on the old Walker place

At the time of Carter's death, his sons, John, Will, and Collins were living at home. With them lived Laura Linda, Martha Adcock's daughter, age 18, and Madora, Albert Adcock's daughter, age 14. Life was now much different in the house that Carter Adcock built on Sycamore Creek.

Living down the road, in the home of William and Lucy Davidson, was Lucy's brother, William Darby, age 20. William's younger brother, Benjamin S. Darby, lived in Nashville. These two men would have a destructive and heartbreaking impact on the Adcock family in the years ahead.

# Chapter Five

## Transition

### (1877-1881)

The world had changed much since Carter and Adelia were married in 1817. Most of the Indians had been removed to reservations west of the Mississippi. The country had suffered through the Civil War. Nashville had grown from about 2,000 people in 1817 to nearly 40,000 people in 1877. Eighteen states had been added to the Union. Carter and Adelia added thirteen children.

In 1877, Rutherford B. Hayes became the 19th President of the United States. The first telephone was installed in Boston. The last battles were fought with Crazy Horse, Chief Joseph and Sitting Bull. The third Kentucky Derby was held. The outlaws, Frank and Jesse James, moved from Missouri to Tennessee.

The deaths of Carter and Adelia Adcock, in 1877, changed the family in many ways. Most of their children were married with families of their own. This is a good time to check on them and see what was going on in their lives.

Nancy Adcock Barnes and Luther Barnes were living at home in Davidson County, with their daughters, Katie and Dillie. With them was their grandson, Edmond. Edmond was the son of Nathaniel and Melinda Adcock Barnes. Melinda died in 1875 and Nathaniel married Martha Raymer in 1876. Nancy and Luther Barnes took-in young Edmond.

Anderson Adcock, and his wife, Caroline, were living in Robertson County, on Sycamore Creek, with eight of their children; Hessie, Sylvanus, known as Sill, Eveline, known as Edie, Mary Ellen, Caroline, known as Callie, Tyler, Talitha, and Taylor. Their daughter, Missie, had married Henry C. Tate in 1874. Their daughter, Martha Jane, married Sam Baxter in 1872. Albert's and Rosy's son, Ed was living with them. He was ten-years-old.

Robert Adcock and his wife, Polly, were living in Robertson County, with seven of their children, Carter E., John Franklin., Cordelia, Mary Ida, Lemmie, Hen and Gip. Their children ranged in age from five to twenty. They were still mourning the loss of their beautiful daughter, Melinda, who died in 1875, at the age of twenty.

Franklin Adcock and his wife, Nancy Jane, were living in Davidson County, with five children, Annie, Almeda, Elizabeth, Edward F. and their infant boy, Carrington Jackson Adcock, whom they called Bibb. Bibb was born on August 29, 1877, between the deaths of Adelia and Carter.

Cynthia Adcock Williams and C.J. Williams were living on Underwood Avenue in Nashville in 1877. With them was their daughter, Elizabeth, who was fifteen. C.J. was listed in the City Directory as a rag dealer.

John C. Adcock was forty-three and single. He was living in the house that his father, Carter, built. Living with him were his brothers Will and Collins. Also living in the house was Laura, the eighteen-year-old daughter of Martha Adcock, and Madora, the fourteen-year-old daughter of Albert and Rosy Adcock.

Martha Matilda Adcock Hatfield and John W. Hatfield had moved from Cedar Hill, in Robertson County, to Montgomery County. Living with them were their sons, John, age eleven, Albert, age nine, and James, age six. They also had three daughters, Mary, age seven, Dillie, age three, and their infant girl, Fanny.

Elizabeth Adcock Cooper's husband, James, died on April 2, 1876. When Elizabeth's parents died, she was living in Davidson County, with her children, William, Mary, James, Elizabeth, and Emma.

Morris Riley Adcock was thirty-seven-years-old when his parents died in 1877. He and his wife, Mary Francis Smiley Adcock, had three children, David, Collins, and Will.

Mary Francis Adcock Smiley and David Smiley were living in Robertson County. With them were their children Lewis, James, Carter, and Albert.

Collins Adcock, who was living in the old homestead with his brothers, John and Will, appeared in county court in 1879. "Collins Adcock, a citizen of the 24th District, this day produced in open Court 3 fox scalps with both ears attached and satisfied the Court that the animals to which they belonged were killed in this County during the past twelve months. It is therefore ordered that the Clerk of this Court issue to said Adcock a certificate for $1.50 to be used by him in the payment of his taxes agreeably to Acts 1879 of General Assembly."

Such bounties on predatory animals were not uncommon. Many states had such laws. They were intended to reduce populations of wild animals that killed and ate livestock and poultry. In Tennessee, the law was revised in 1896, raising the bounty to $2 per animal. Foxes no longer qualified, but wolves and panthers did. The law read, "Any person killing wolves or panthers in the State, upon application to the county court with proper proofs, may receive a certificate from the court entitling him to a bounty of $2 for each animal, which certificate may be applied on the payment of State and county taxes not to exceed one-half the total tax of the person."

The family slowly adjusted to the loss of Albert and Rosy and the loss of Carter and Adelia. As time passed, life on the farms along Sycamore Creek returned to the normal routine. Mary Frances and David Smiley had a son, David C. Smiley, born May 7, 1878. Riley and Mary Frances Adcock had another son. Morris Riley Adcock was born on May 28, 1878.

Carter's and Adelia's son, Robert Adcock, died on January 21, 1880, of pneumonia at his home in Robertson County. He had been very ill and requested William Smiley, J.W. Nichols and J.W. Pyle to come to his house and witness his Last Will and Testament. In it he named his seven living children, Carter Edward Adcock, John Franklin Adcock, Cordelia Ann Adcock, Mary Ida Adcock, Lem Izer "Lemmie" Adcock, Robert Henderson "Hen" Adcock and Gip Taylor Adcock.

Polly Railey Adcock and her sons, Hen and Gip

Robert wanted his real and personal property to remain in the possession of his wife, Polly Ann Railey Adcock during her lifetime. At her death, his property was to be divided equally among his children. He added an interesting item to his will. He stated, "I have another heir which I wish to will one dollar. That is Edmond Barnes."

Edmund Samuel Barnes, Robert Adcock's grandson, was the son of his daughter, Melinda Adcock. Melinda Adcock married Robert Nathaniel Barnes on March 21, 1872. Robert Nathaniel Barnes was the son of Luther Barnes and Nancy Adcock Barnes. Edmond Barnes was born on February 2, 1873. Malinda died about 1875, so she was not named in her father's will. On December 14, 1876, Robert Nathaniel Barnes married Martha Ann Pamela Raymer. When Robert Adcock died, in 1880, Edmund Samuel Barnes was living with his other grandparents, Luther Barnes and Nancy Adcock Barnes.

The 1880 Federal Census says Martha Adcock Hatfield was living with her husband and six children in Montgomery County. This census lists John Hatfield's occupation as wheelwright. Carter's and Adelia's daughter, Martha, died in August, 1881. We know this from court testimony from her daughter, Laura Adcock Darby.

# Chapter Six

## The Darby Brothers and Dark Days Ahead

Laura Adcock was the daughter of Martha Adcock and an unknown man. She lived with her grandparents, Carter and Adelia Adcock. After they died, in 1877, she lived in the same house with her uncles John, Will and Collins and her cousin, Madora Adcock. On November 17, 1881, Laura Adcock married Benjamin S. Darby. Benjamin lived with his sister, Mary Bradley, on Demonbreun Street, in Nashville.

It is likely that Laura met Benjamin through his brother, William Darby, who lived with his sister, Lucy Davidson, near the Adcock home on Sycamore Creek. Benjamin, worked in Nashville as a yard man for the NC&StL Railroad.

Benjamin's brother, William Darby, began seeing Madora Adcock, the daughter of Albert and Rosy Adcock. On December 13, 1885, Madora married William Darby. She was twenty-years-old. William was twenty-five. Laura's husband, Benjamin Darby, vanished from the public record about this time.

Dr. John Bainbridge had been a friend of the Adcock family for many years. He lived nearby. He attended Albert and Rosy Adcock before they died. He was born about 1816 and was married to Mary J. Bugg. They had eight children. Mary died in 1884. On April 27, 1886, Laura Adcock Darby married Dr. John Bainbridge. He was about seventy-years-old. Laura was about twenty-four.

Marriage License for Dr. John Bainbridge and Laura Adcock Darby

The lives of almost every member of the Adcock family changed on May 22, 1886, when William and Madora Darby filed a lawsuit over the inheritance of Madora and Ed. The lawsuit was filed against their guardian, and uncle, Franklin Adcock, et al. That "et al" is significant. It means, "and others." In this case, it seemed to mean anyone named Adcock or anyone married to, or friends of, an Adcock.

As the orphan daughter of Albert and Rosy Adcock, Madora had been taken-in by her grandparents. She would have been provided for like any other member of the family. After her grandparents died, Madora grew up in the household with her three uncles, John, Will and Collins, and older cousin, Laura, on Sycamore Creek. Shortly after she married William Darby, he initiated a lawsuit to recover the money left to her and her brother, Ed Adcock, by their parents.

Because both Madora and Ed were minor children when their parents died, the court had appointed their uncle, Franklin, to look after their inheritance. It was a nice inheritance of around a thousand dollars. That would be around $22,000 in today's money.

From the many pages of testimony, it is clear that Franklin never intended to deprive Madora and Ed of their inheritance. The truth is that Franklin was not qualified to manage money. He actually claimed that he didn't want to be appointed guardian for Madora's and Ed's estate. No doubt, he used their inheritance for his own purposes. Franklin engaged in loans, land purchases, and complicated land swaps. These deals involved many friends and family members. The court tried to follow the money. Because the investments, loans and land transfers were so complicated, the process took years to complete. A great deal happened during those years.

Madora's brother, Ed Adcock, was only three-years-old when his parents died. Ed was taken in by his uncle and aunt, Anderson and Caroline Adcock. Ed was living with Anderson and Caroline in 1880. When the lawsuit was filed, Ed had recently turned nineteen years old.

From the day the court case was filed until it was finally resolved, the family was torn apart. Over those years, friends and family were forced to testify for and against each other. The transcripts of the various court appearances are full of frustration, anger and bitterness. The case left scars that never healed.

When the court appointed Franklin Adcock as guardian for Madora and Ed Adcock, he had to post a bond. The purpose of the bond was to insure that the minor children of Albert and Rosy Adcock were protected in case something happened to Franklin or their inheritance. Signing the bond with Franklin were his father, Carter Adcock, and a friend, I. R. Reeder. The first paragraph of the guardian document reads as follows:

State of Tennessee

Know all men by these presents, That we Franklin Adcock, Carter Adcock, and I.R. Reeder all of Davidson County in the State aforesaid, are held and firmly bound unto the State of Tennessee in the sum of Two Thousand Five Hundred Dollars, to be paid to the said State, in trust, for the benefit of the wards hereafter named, committed to the tuition of the said Franklin Adcock to which payment, well and truly to be made, we bind ourselves and each of us, each and every one of our heirs, executors and administrators, jointly and severally, firmly, by these presents. Sealed with our seals, and dated the 23rd day of February 1872.

The attorneys for William Darby, his wife, Madora, and Madora's brother, wanted to be sure they collected money for their clients. So, they included Carter Adcock and I. R. Reeder, in an effort to collect from them, as they had signed Franklin's bond as guardian. As we know, Carter Adcock died before the Darby lawsuit was filed. That is why all of Carter's children, as heirs to his estate, were named in the lawsuit. In the cases where Carter's children had died, their children, even those who were minors, were sued. The case was "Wm Darby and wife, et al vs Franklin Adcock, et al." Et al, indeed!

We will not attempt to write a complete history of the trial. It would be difficult. Much of it is repetitive and tedious declarations made by lawyers, but some of the testimony is illuminating. It is a rare opportunity to hear the spoken words of these members of the Adcock family, even though they were spoken under difficult circumstances.

We understand why Franklin Adcock was the focus of the trial. His situation is clearly established in the following testimony on April 24, 1888:

> Q. State your age, residence and occupation.
>
> A. I am 63 years old, live in Robertson County. I am a farmer.
>
> Q. Were you or not the Guardian of Medora Darby and Edward Adcock?
>
> A. I was.
>
> Q. The copy of the bond shows you signed it on February 23, 1872, when did you get the guardian fund from whom did you get it and how much did you get?
>
> A. I don't recollect whether it was right at the date of the bond or not, but it could not have been but few days afterwards. I got it from Riley Adcock, administrator of Albert Adcock deceased. It was one thousand and sixteen and 40/100 dollars.

Nancy Adcock Barnes and her husband, Luther, were named as defendants. We have not found any testimony by her. It appears she was only named because she was the daughter of Carter Adcock. This also appears to be the case for Carter's sons, Anderson, John, Will and Collins.

Carter's son, Robert Adcock, died in 1880, long before the lawsuit was filed. Because Carter had signed the guardianship bond with Franklin Adcock, and because Franklin had loaned to Robert some of the money that was Mardora's and Ed's inheritance, Robert's children were named in the lawsuit. The trial documents state the following:

> He [Carter Adcock] had a son, Robert Adcock who is dead, and left the following children and heirs at law viz, Defendants, Delia Smiley, Ida Adcock, Carter Adcock, John Adcock, Henderson Adcock, Taylor Adcock, and Louisa Adcock.

What Franklin said in court, during the trial, gives some idea of how complicated his dealings were, and how difficult it became to figure out where the money went. The following testimony describes a small loan Franklin made to his brother, Robert Adcock.

> Q. How much of the guardian fund did you loan to Robert Adcock.
>
> A. $150.
>
> Q. When did you loan it to him, and how long did he keep it?
>
> A. A few months after I got it, and about 6 or 7 years after, I took a mule at $100 and after that, balance in money in about two payments.
>
> Q. Did you or not hold the mule as the property of your wards?
>
> A. Of course, I did.
>
> Q. What did you do with the mule?
>
> A. I sold it to Parrish for $90 and took his note.
>
> Q. What did you do with the Parrish note?
>
> A. Paid it on the land.
>
> Q. Did you use any of the money Robert Adcock paid you on the land?
>
> A. Nothing but the mule.

This passage from testimony gives some insight to Franklin Adcock. Asked about another mule he got in payment for a note he held from John Raley, Franklin answered as follows:

Q. What did you do with the mule?

A. I sold him for $120.

Q. What did you do with the $120 you got for the mule?

A. That ain't a fair question.

Q. Now, what did you do with that money?

A. I made use of it, buying bread with it. I paid my tax out of it, and got away with it one way and another.

Q. When did you sell the mule?

A. Over a year ago.

Q. Where did you sell him at? I mean what place?

A. Nashville.

Q. What did you do with the money you got from John Raley?

A. I made use of it. My recollection ain't sufficient now to tell what I did with it.

Q. What property have you now?

A. I have very little. I have two cows and calves, two mares, a few sheep, fifteen or sixteen head, one hundred acres of land, besides this you are working after, a few hogs and household furniture.

Cynthia Adcock Williams, and her husband, C.J. Williams are very much involved in the lawsuit. Franklin loaned them money from the inheritance of Madora and Ed Adcock to buy property in Nashville. They used the money to by Lots 25 and 26 in the Underwood development in Nashville. The Nashville City Directories from 1879 through 1882, show that C.J. and Cynthia Williams were living on Underwood Avenue near Hawthorn Street.

Those lots were sold by C.J. and Cynthia Williams to Fisk University. Some of the money from that sale went to purchase 208 acres of land from I.N. and J.T. Pyles, near Sycamore Creek. That land was divided and deeded to Cynthia Williams, Franklin's sister, and Jane Adcock, Franklin's wife. The deed to 104 acres of that land was put in Cynthia's name. In a deposition on April 25, 1888, C. J. Williams responded to questions regarding the 104 acres:

Q. What is your age, residence and occupation and are you one of the defendants to this cause and the husband of defendant Cynthia Williams?

A. I am 57 years old, live in this county and I am a farmer. I am the husband of the defendant Cynthia Williams and am a defendant to this cause.

Q. When did Franklin Adcock buy the Pyles land, and if you or your wife now own any of it, how much, and when did you move on it, and has a deed been executed to your wife for it? If so, when was deed executed?

A. He bought the land about the 3$^{rd}$ day of March, 1884. My wife owns 104 acres of it. She has a deed to it executed on the 5$^{th}$ day of March 1886. We moved on it the 20$^{th}$ day of April 1883.

Franklin Adcock had purchased 208 acres of land from the Pyles brothers. The other 104 acres was deeded to his wife, Jane Adcock. In testimony on April 26, 1888, she said she knew all about the money from the sale of lots in Nashville to Fisk University. She said her husband used the money to buy land from the Pyles brothers.

Q. After this did or not your husband take any money? If so how much did he take and what did he say he was going to do with it?

A. He did. $600. He said he was going to take it and finish paying for the Pyles' land.

Q. Did you ever hear C.J. Williams say anything about owing Albert Adcock's heirs? If so, what did he say?

A. I have heard say several times that he didn't deny his indebtedness to that estate.

Q. Did you or not ever hear him say anything about your husband going off or leaving the state or being arrested? If so, what did he say?

A. He said that Franklin had better go away awhile and if he (Williams) did succeed in getting the place, he would do all he could in making bread for his [Franklin Adcock's] children.

The children of Martha Adcock Hatfield were named in the lawsuit. This deposition by Laura Adcock Bainbridge was taken at the home of Dr. John Bainbridge in Nashville, on May 4, 1888.

Q. Are you the wife of Dr. John Bainbridge?

A. I am.

Q. What relation were you to Martha Hatfield?

A. Daughter.

Q. When did your mother die?

A. In August, 1881.

Q. What were the names of her children?

A. Myself, John Hatfield, Mary Hatfield, Albert Hatfield, James Hatfield, Dillie Hatfield, and Fanny Hatfield.

Elizabeth Adcock Cooper, sister of Albert Adcock, figures prominently in this case, but not in the way you might expect. She appears at a critical event that occurred during the trial. Not long after the lawsuit began, Madora gave birth to a baby girl. On October 12, 1886, Laura Genora Darby was born. A few weeks later, on December 20, 1886, Madora died. Elizabeth Cooper, who was called "Bettie" began caring for the baby, Laura, when she was only two months old. On November 2, 1887, William Darby gave up the child to be adopted by her great aunt, Elizabeth. She became Laura Genora Cooper.

When William Darby gave up his daughter for adoption, he also signed over to Elizabeth Adcock Cooper, any and all of his share in the inheritance of his deceased wife, Madora Adcock Darby.

Registered Nov 2, 1887

The following agreement is hereby made and entered into this first day of November 1887 by and between Wm. Darby of the first part and Elizabeth L Cooper of the second part.

1st It is agreed by the said Elizabeth L. Cooper that she will take the child of the said Wm Darby, namely Laura Darby, an infant, and will adopt the same as her child and will rear, support, and educate it as far as lies in her power and her means and those hereafter given her will permit and at her death will see that said child has an equal portion of her property with her own children and that such part of the fund herein after mentioned not fully expended at her death to go to said child Laura Darby.

2nd In consideration of the foregoing the said Wm Darby on his part hereby gives to the said Elizabeth L. Cooper all money coming to him in the case of Laura Darby et al vs Franklin Adcock et al pending in the Chancery Court of Robertson County, State of Tennessee, except a sufficiency of the same to pay the attorney's fees and other proper charges against the same and an account due Dr. John L Bainbridge for $28.76 with interest from September 26, 1886 and he herein sells and assigns to her all his rights and interest in said case and by this paper directs the Clerk and Master or his attorneys to pay the same to said Elizabeth L Cooper. Witness our hands this 1 day of November 1887.

The document is signed by William Darby and Elizabeth L Cooper.[4]

To get an idea of all the people affected by William Darby's actions, consider the following list of defendants:

To the Honorable George E. Seay Chancellor and holding the Chancery Court at Springfield, Tennessee.

William Darby and his wife, Medora Darby and Edward Adcock all citizens of Davidson County, Tennessee, who sue as here in after stated Bring this Bill Against:

Franklin Adcock, I. R. Reeder, Jas Spain and his wife Mrs. Mary Spain, Richard Spain, C. J. Williams and wife Cynthia Williams, Jane Adcock, Anderson Adcock, Riley Adcock, Mary Smiley and husband David Smiley, Delia Smiley and husband Seb Smiley, Carter Adcock, John Adcock, Henderson Adcock, Taylor Adcock, Louisa Adcock, Citizens of Robertson County Tennessee, William Adcock, John Adcock, Collins Adcock, Mrs. Elizabeth Cooper, Dr. John Bainbridge and wife, Laura Bainbridge, Citizens of Davidson County Tennessee. Nancy Barnes and husband Luther Barnes, citizens of Cheatham County, Tennessee and Booker Raley and wife Ida Raley, John Hatfield, Mary Hatfield Adcock, Albert Hatfield, James Hatfield, Dillie Hatfield, Fannie Hatfield, all Citizens of the State of Kentucky.

We have given only a small portion of the trial. We read over 340 hand-written legal size pages of testimony related to this lawsuit. Some important information came from an amendment to the original lawsuit. In that amendment, more complications arose for Collins Adcock. Names of friends and neighbors of Franklin were added as defendants.

On November 30, 1886 Darby's lawyers filed an amendment to their original lawsuit in Chancery Court in Springfield. The lawyers said that, since the original filing of the lawsuit, they had learned that Carter Adcock, who co-signed the bond for Franklin Adcock as the guardian of minors Madora and Ed Adcock, was a resident of Robertson County, and not Davidson County, as originally stated. On February 18, 1882, an attorney named Ed Gannaway, had been appointed as administrator of Carter Adcock by the Davidson County Court. Gannaway had filed a Bill against some of the heirs of Carter Adcock to sell a tract of 174 acres of land to pay a debt of $87.50 and interest since 1875.

On July 22, 1882, Collins Adcock placed a bid of $1,375 for the 174 acre tract. On August 13, 1883, the land was ordered to be sold because the children of Martha Adcock Hatfield had not been included in the Bill filed by Ed Gannaway, and because Collins had only made one payment of $275 for the land. He refused to sell the land or acknowledge ownership of it because the court wanted the land, or the money for the land, set aside and possibly paid to William Darby, Madora and Ed

---

[4] This adoption document is located in the Davidson County Contract Deeds book 107, page 121

Adcock.

To complicate matters even more, Franklin Adcock, according to the amended Bill, had been "cutting timber off and otherwise committing waste on the land." Darby's attorneys ask for an injunction to keep Franklin from cutting any more timber on the 174 acre tract. The also asked that the Court order the sale of the 174 acres to benefit William and Madora Darby and Ed Adcock.

Another land transaction included in the lawsuit devastated I.R. Reeder and his daughter, Mary A. Spain. This land became part of the lawsuit because I.R. Reeder had also signed the bond for Franklin Adcock as guardian of Albert's two children.

Franklin Adcock had purchased 208 acres of land from I.N. Pyles and J.T. Pyles. He used money held in trust for Albert's children to pay for the land.

In the end, the judge concluded that Franklin Adcock had failed to do what was right regarding the inheritance of his brother's orphaned children, Madora and Ed Adcock. On May 4, 1888, the judge wrote, "In brief; it appears that the only things he did was collect the money of his wards and proceeded to use it for his own purposes." The verdict was that Franklin Adcock owed the amount of the inheritance with interest compounded from 1872. The total amount due Madora and Ed was $2,704.12.

Of course, Franklin didn't have the money to pay what the court had ordered. It would be good to say that the judge's decision was the end of this long painful episode, but it was not. In 1894, eight years after the lawsuit was filed, land was still being sold on the courthouse steps to satisfy the debt. Relationships among members of the family never recovered. Some of the children of John and Martha Adcock Hatfield moved to Kentucky. Friends of Franklin lost money, land, and their trust in him. It is possible that the stress contributed to Madora's death. It certainly contributed to Jane's decision to leave her husband, Franklin.

# Chapter Seven

## Laura's Story

In the previous chapter, you read about the devastating effect the Darby vs. Adcock lawsuit had on the Adcock family and their friends and neighbors. Sometimes, it is good to step back and look at a story from a different perspective. In this chapter, we wanted to follow the story of little Laura Darby to show that even when things appear dark, there is always hope.

Laura's story is both heartbreaking and reaffirming. It is a compelling story that begins long before she was born on October 24, 1886. It all began with the sudden and premature deaths of her grandparents, Albert and Rosanna Oaks Adcock.

Albert and Rosanna were married in Nashville, Tennessee, on March 22, 1865. They made their home near Albert's parents, Carter and Adelia Adcock, and started a family. Their first child, Madora, was born in 1865. Their son, Edward, arrived in 1867.

Around 1870, Albert died. Two days later, Rosanna died. There is no documentation that reveals the exact date or cause of their death. Albert was about thirty years old. Rosanna was only twenty-two. They left behind two small children, Madora "Dora", who was five years old, and Edward "Ed", who was three years old.

Riley Adcock, Albert's younger brother, was appointed administrator of the estate. He sold everything that Albert owned, paid all of his debts, including three doctors' bills, and held the remainder, consisting of cash, gold, and silver valued at $1,016.80.

Franklin Adcock, another of Albert's brothers, was appointed guardian. Carter Adcock and I. R. Reeder signed a $2,500.00 bond to secure the guardianship. Riley turned all of the money over to Franklin so that a trust could be set up for Dora and Ed. Neither of Albert's two minor children ever lived with Franklin. Ed lived with Albert's older brother, Anderson, and his wife, Caroline Adcock. Dora lived with her grandparents, Carter and Adelia.

Carter and Adelia already had another granddaughter living with them when Dora moved there. Laura Adcock, the daughter of Martha Adcock Hatfield, was nine years old. Even though she was four years older than Dora, Laura and Dora became very close friends.

When Laura was twenty years old, she married Benjamin Darby. They were married on November 17, 1881. Benjamin had a younger brother named William. William was born on August 3, 1860. Benjamin and William immigrated from Horncastle, England, with their family in 1877. On December 13, 1885,

Dora and William Darby were married in Davidson County, TN. She was twenty years old.

Five months after Dora and William were married, William Darby filed a lawsuit as "next kin" of Dora and Ed. The lawsuit, filed on May 22, 1886, was against Franklin for the trust fund money of $1,016.80. A minor could not file a lawsuit; therefore, it had to be filed by someone who was at least 21 years old as their "next kin". This lawsuit lasted for more than eight years and involved all of Carter's children, some of his grandchildren, and others in the area. It caused tension and hardship on everyone involved.

On October 24, 1886, Dora gave birth to a daughter she named Laura Genora Darby. Obviously, she was named in honor of Dora's cousin, Laura. On December 20, 1886, when baby Laura was less than two months old, her mother died. There is no documentation to tell what happened to her. We do know from court records that there was a charge from Dr. John Bainbridge in September 1886, a month before Laura was born. This could indicate that Dora was not well during the end of her pregnancy. It appears that Dora took care of her baby, Laura, until she died. Dora's Aunt Elizabeth Adcock Cooper, Albert's sister, took care of baby Laura from the time Laura was two months old.

Bettie Cooper's husband, James "Jim" Cooper, died April 2, 1876, leaving Bettie with five children and a small farm in the Forest Grove community of Davidson County, Tennessee. On November 1, 1887, William Darby and Elizabeth L. Cooper entered into a legal contract which gave custody of Laura to Bettie Cooper. The contract gave Bettie all money coming to him in the case of Laura Darby vs. Franklin Adcock, except any amounts due attorneys and court fees, and the amount due to Dr. Bainbridge, plus interest. It also stated that Bettie would take the child and adopt her and rear, support, and educate her, and, at Bettie's death, the child would have an equal portion of her property just as Bettie's other children. It further stated that such part of the trust fund money, if any was left after raising the child, would go to Laura.

On July 30, 1888, William Darby petitioned the court and received his United States citizenship. On October 30, 1888, Laura petitioned the court for the adoption of Laura. The petition stated that Bettie had become very much attached to Laura. It also stated that, "the child's father is of peculiar disposition, does not care for the child as a parent usually does, shows no special affection for her and what money he makes he is very imprudent with it, never lays by anything and is not likely to do so, and does not contribute anything for the child's support being more or less addicted to drinking intoxicants". On November 5, 1888, Bettie was granted the adoption and Laura's last name was changed to Cooper.

Laura, after she was adopted by Bettie Cooper

The 1900 Federal Census shows Laura was thirteen. She lived with her mother, Elizabeth Cooper, on the farm. She had attended school and seemed to have a good childhood.

The year 1905 brought about a huge change in Laura's life. On Christmas Eve, she became the wife of Willie Grandville Towns. Laura was 19 years old. Willie was twenty-seven. He grew up in the same community as Laura. His mother was Tempy Ward, and his father was Henry Towns. Willie registered for the draft on September 12, 1918. He listed his wife, Laura, and his occupation as a farmer. He was described as slender and short with brown hair and blue eyes.

At the time Willie registered for the WWI draft, he and Laura had six children; Roscoe, born March 4, 1908, Dorothy, born November 30, 1910, Ruby Florence, born May 5, 1912, Willie, born December

20, 1914, Brownie, born September 22, 1915, and, Norman, who was called "Buck", born September 15, 1917.

A man gave one of the children a French horn and all of the children delighted in playing with it. From it, they all contracted Tuberculosis. Roscoe died from the disease one day after his twentieth birthday, on March 5, 1928. His brother, Brownie died of the disease on July 23, 1942, at the age of twenty-six.

World War I ended on November 11, 1918. Four more children were born to Laura and Willie after the war. Hazel was born on June 19, 1919, Lucille on June 16, 1921, Lawrence, known as "Sparks" on March 10, 1924, and, Geraldine, who was called "Dink" on January 10, 1927.

Laura's husband, Willie, died on August 14, 1938, from cancer of the throat and face. They had been married a little over thirty-two years. After Willie's death, Laura lived in several locations in Nashville, with her children, Sparks and Dink.

Lawrence "Sparks" Towns enlisted in the Navy in WWII. He served as a machinist mate 3rd class, aboard the Destroyer Underhill. His ship was attacked and sunk on July 24, 1945. Sparks was wounded and received a Purple Heart. He died on January 19, 2017, at the age of ninety-two.

Laura's son, Norman, died on October 24, 1993. Laura's daughters; Geraldine "Dink" died on July 7, 1990, Hazel, died at Whites Creek on February 9, 1996, Ruby Florence, died on October 16, 1995, and is buried in the Webb Cemetery in Joelton, and, Lucille died in 1997. Laura's son, Willie, died on October 16, 1998.

Dorothy Towns Lain, daughter of Laura, died on March 16, 1996. She was the mother of Barbara, the little girl pictured in the next photograph with her grandmother, Laura. Carolyn Adcock-Smith had the pleasure of talking with Barbara recently. She remembered her "Grandmamma" very well. She always loved to visit her in Nashville. They would go to Centennial Park on picnics and downtown to hear live music.

Barbara and her grandmother, Laura Genora Darby Cooper Towns


Laura's story could have been much different. The tragic and divisive events leading up to her birth could have put her on a bad road. The intervention of a loving aunt, changed that. Laura had a happy marriage and gave birth to eleven children. She lived a long and productive life. Laura died on September 26, 1973, in Nashville. She was eighty-six. She is buried in the Webb Cemetery in Joelton, Tennessee, beside Willie.

# Chapter Eight

# Turn of a Century

# (1900 – 1919)

The Darby vs. Adcock lawsuit fractured the family. There is no denying that. But, other factors also caused the various lines of the family to go in different directions. This often happens when the old generation dies off. The bond that held them all together is broken. From this point forward, we focus on the family line of Carter's and Adelia's son, Morris Riley Adcock.

You might think the area surrounding Sycamore Creek was inhabited only by farmers at the end of the 19th Century. A look at occupations listed on Federal Census records from the period is illuminating. Among the various jobs are timber merchant, blacksmith, gunsmith, miller, seamster, grocer, paper maker, shoe maker, wagon maker, saddle maker, wood cutter, school teacher, midwife, constable, stone mason, carpenter, and even one gold miner. But most, by far, were farmers.

Riley Adcock was a farmer and blacksmith. His wife, Mary Frances Smiley, was born in Robertson County, Tennessee, on January 15, 1840. Her father was Samuel Smiley and her mother was Hessie Ann Warren. Following her family line back in time, we know that her paternal grandfather was David Smiley, one of the early settlers of Ridgetop. David was born in Derry, in County Cavan, Ireland, in 1780. He died on September 17, 1860. His wife, Temperance, was born in North Carolina, in 1780. She died in 1858.

A plaque, honoring David and Temperance Smiley at the Love Cemetery at Ridgetop.

Mary's maternal grandparents were Sebert Asher Warren and Frances Bushrod Swift. They married in Robertson County, Tennessee, on March 9, 1810. Sebert was born in Richmond, Virginia, on July 2, 1790. He served in the 2nd Regiment of the West Tennessee Militia in the War of 1812. Sebert died on September 12, 1863, in Bolivar, Missouri. Frances was born on June 2, 1791, in Caswell, North Carolina. She died on September 13, 1865, at Walnut Hill, Illinois. She is buried at Shook Cemetery in Marion County, Illinois.

We know some things about Mary from stories written by her daughter-in-law, Annie Biggs Adcock. Annie Biggs moved with her family from Cheatham County to Robertson County in 1901. She was nine-years-old. Her family lived very close to the home of Riley and Mary Adcock.

Mary Smiley Adcock by Annie Biggs Adcock

Mary Smiley Adcock, my husband's mother, was a fine housekeeper. She spun thread on a spinning wheel and made all their socks. They had sheep and they sheared the wool and washed it, carded it, and made little rolls about a half a foot long out of the wool and spun it into thread on the spinning wheel. I had never heard one before and it scared me half crazy. I ran home and got my mamma and we went to see what it was. We came to where she was spinning on the back porch. I thought it was a terrible sight. Later, I saw her knitting with four, what she called, knit needles. She made them all two pair of socks apiece. I don't until this day know how she done it, as she doubled the heels and toes of socks. She pieced quilts and quilted from three to four new quilts every fall. There was no end to their work.

They didn't can very much but there was no end to drying apples and sliced pumpkins. They killed hogs and saved every one of the entrails to make soap. Not as we make soap. They saved all ashes from the fireplace and the cook stove and put them in an old ash hopper. The ash hopper was a log about eight feet long, split with a trench down through the middle. It was higher at one end than the other just a little. There was a row of planks nailed on each side of the log. They covered this to keep rain out. They filled it with hickory wood ashes. Just before they got ready to make soap, they would run the water over top of these ashes, let it run down the log into the pot, or whatever they had to catch it in. The ashes had rotted and made the finest red lye you ever looked at. They smoked the hog entrails and they cooked them in this lye and you ought to have seen the soap. They never bought no soap or soap powder.

They also raised geese. The creek bottoms were full of geese. They picked them and made feather beds and pillows. They had some of the prettiest pillows and feather beds I ever saw.

The family of Riley and Mary Adcock consisted of four boys. One, whose name was Collins, died when he was twenty-one-years-old. The other three lived to be older. Dave was the oldest one of them. Will was the next, and then Collins, who died young. Then, the youngest one was Morris Riley Adcock, Jr.

Mary Smiley Adcock died on September 19, 1909. She is buried at Forest Grove Cemetery in Joelton, Tennessee.

Another story by Annie Biggs Adcock, gives us a first-hand account of the area around Sycamore Creek between 1901 and 1919. It was not open land as it is now. It was a busy community. It was more accurately described as a settlement.

The Perry brothers, Wash and John, moved from Cheatham County to the edge of Robertson County, near Sycamore Creek, in the 1890s. They both had large families and built houses on the bank of Sycamore Creek. The Perry brothers were the first to start tobacco farming in the area. They helped to build Bethel Church of Christ. The congregation met, for a while, in a small log building at the intersection of Whites Creek Pike and Greenbrier Road. Some of the pioneer families in the congregation included Sexton, Gentry, Perry, Huffman, Waits, Towns, Williams, Knight, and Spain. For a time, they had gospel meetings in a barn, owned by John Perry. In 1895, a frame building was constructed on the site where a newer church now stands.

Bethel Church of Christ built in 1895

The Perry houses were about two miles back from the Springfield Road (now White's Creek Pike). The road to Springfield or Nashville was a dirt road. There were no bridges across the creek, so when there was a big rain, that meant no crossing the creek.

The next home up the Ridge from the Perry brothers, was Joe Spain's place on top of the hill from the creek. There was another family that lived at the fork in that road. The road was known as Webb Road. It is now Coopertown Road. At that place, there was a little country store run by Ben Waits.

The next house up the road was the Drake's home. It was used as a tavern during the Civil War. Will Mayo's home was next, later known as the George Bracy home. A short distance further on was the old Felts' home. The next building was the old Forest Grove Methodist Church, which was built around 1870.

Across from the church is a lane leading back to Forest Grove Cemetery. Dick Lane and his wife, Lucy Hobbs Lane, lived in a big log house at the back of the cemetery. On the cemetery property was a one-room log building. It was the first school in the area.

In 1901, my father, William Carrol Biggs and our family, left the Big Marrowbone near Mount Pleasant Baptist Church, in Cheatham County, and moved to Sycamore Creek. It was a deeply wooded area at that time, with few houses, and very far apart. We moved in an old house facing the creek, called the Seats House.

Old man Seats was a drunkard, and he would beat his wife every time he got drunk. They didn't have no children. One evening he came home drunk and beat his wife up, and sat down in a chair and went to sleep. His wife took a notion she had taken enough of these beatings. So, she got the chopping axe, which they said must have been sharp, slipped up where he had thrown his head back across the chair back. She come down on him with this sharp axe and chopped off his head.

There was blood all over the top of the room where he jumped up and hit the top of the room. Well, they had to bury him in a wooden box. They carried him out this old road on a slide pulled by oxen to what they called the Old Liberty Graveyard. The so-called law at that time give the old woman ten days to leave the county. And she did, and was never seen again by anybody in this area.

We was always wondering, us children that is, if we would see or hear Old Seats, since we moved in the old house. But, I never heard nothing.

On the Springfield Road, near the road to Sycamore Creek, lived a preacher named George Milliken with his wife, Nannie. Across from his home was a small country store owned by Henry E. Demonbreun.

Besides my dad and my mother, Julia Ann Capps Biggs, there were five of us children. There was Jack, Minnie, me, Mattie, and Mary. When we went to church, we had to walk, unless we caught a ride in a surrey with one of the families who lived along Springfield Road.

The first paved road on the Ridge came in 1903, or 1904. There was only a narrow dirt road all the way to the top of the Ridge at Joelton, all around through Eaton's Creek Road and Germantown. Sometimes they were so muddy you could hardly go. People was complaining everywhere. They decided to have a road speaking at a bend in Sycamore Creek called the Turn Hole, They barbecued pork and sheep and had a wonderful dinner. Everybody brought something. They had some fine cooks in them days who brought just about everything. I was small, but I remember it all.

They had a bunch of people from the Nashville Courthouse to come and make a speech. They knew it would raise taxes, but, at that time you could not hardly get to Nashville or Springfield for the bad roads. I never heard such a speaking, or saw as much to eat. All the drink they had was lemonade, at ten cents a glass. It was made in big lard cans.

They decided on the road. They brought the rock from Peggy Holler, which lays to the back of Forest Grove Church, about 3/4 of a mile. Peggy Holler got its name from a cabin up on the hill, called the old Peggy Teague hut. Folks said she had a wash kettle full of money buried up there somewhere in them ditches. She died nearly 100 years ago, but the old hut is still partly there, and the treasure hunt still in progress.

They blasted out the rock and had the road widened out. They covered the road from here to Joelton, with about one half foot of blue flint rock. They moved a rock crusher down there and ground fine rock to go over the rough rock. It was run on steam. We called the big machine a "whillopowhalipor." That's the sounds it made.

They hauled the rock with wagons and mules. Everybody who had mules and a wagon helped. The ones who didn't have a wagon helped to load the rock.

When the road was finished, we thought we had the finest community ever. Of course those of us who lived back from this road had a hard time getting to it. If the men had a load to take to town, they took out part of it to the big road and unloaded the wagon. Then, they went back after the rest.

Riley Adcock was living on Sycamore Creek with his wife, Mary, and his four sons, when the Biggs family moved there from Cheatham County, in 1901. He was a blacksmith. He farmed a little, too. There was always a crowd at his blacksmith shop, which sat beside Sycamore Creek. Horses and mules had to be shod. Plows and hoes had to be sharpened.

When he could, he went hunting. He had a fine coon hound. One story was told about a hunting trip he made about three o'clock one morning. It started when his dog began barking. Riley woke up when he heard his dog barking in the distance. He decided to see what the barking was all about. He didn't wake anyone up, but put on his clothes and slipped out quietly with his gun and a lantern.

He followed the barking sounds for about a mile. They led him past the Reeder Graveyard. As he passed the graveyard, something came out and began walking beside him, every step he made. It walked with him for a long distance and then, disappeared. He continued on to where the dog had a raccoon treed. He shot the raccoon out of the top of the tree. He took the raccoon home and his dog followed. The next day, he told his friends about the hunting trip. He said he figured it was a ghost from that cemetery. Others talked about many strange things that had been seen and heard there.

The Reeder Graveyard is an old place where a bunch of people were buried long ago. But, the ghosts have walked the hills in the territory all these years according to old legends. It is located about a quarter of a mile from Sycamore Creek on the left side of Huffman Road.

One of the Huffman boys was going to church at Bethel Church of Christ one night. It was about eleven when services turned out. He was in an old buggy with no top on it. He had to go by Sycamore Creek and up the hill by Reeder Graveyard. All at once something dipped down over the buggy and got his hat. He got out of there and he never saw his hat again.

Another time, Riley's oldest son, Dave, and one of his neighbors, Will Smith, known as Ras, made plans to go hunting one Sunday morning. They met where they had planned. There had been a shower that settled the dusty road that ran along by this graveyard. They went off the road, beside the cemetery where there were some mulberry trees. They heard squirrels barking up in the trees. They were both marksmen. There was a squirrel, just sitting on a limb. So, Ras told Dave to shoot. That squirrel said, "Oh!" Dave said he never even touched the squirrel. So, Dave told Ras to try his luck. Ras shot. The same thing happened. The squirrel said, "Oh, Ras!"

All at once they heard a surrey coming down the road. The graveyard was between them and the road. This surrey stopped at the graveyard. They heard people talking and they hid for a while, not wanting anyone to see them hunting on Sunday. Everything became quiet. They looked for the squirrel. He was gone.

They went to the graveyard. There was no sign of wagon tracks. There was no sign of anybody's tracks. Dave said it was a mystery. He said he was broke from hunting on Sunday.

Around 1901, Riley's and Mary's son, Will Adcock, married Laura Chambliss. Will was twenty-eight-years-old. Riley's son, Dave, who was thirty-two, had not married, but was courting a nice young woman named Valeria Drake. Riley's youngest son, Morris Riley Adcock, Jr., who was called, Gooden, was twenty-three, and, by several accounts, was very talented and handsome. His future wife, Annie, said, "He was young and full of fun, and wasn't by no means bad looking, with his bright blue eyes and red curly hair, which he wore out long. I never thought nothing about his wearing long hair then. Only that it was pretty."

Annie recalled and occasion she attended in 1902.

> This happened at the old Turn Hole bottoms where the bridge goes up Huffman Road, better known as Dividing Ridge Road, just a little above the small creek called Bednigo. They had fruit stands, about three of them, just a square made of planks and shelves where they had ice cream and cold lemonade, and sandwiches.
>
> There were two big places built about two feet high for the musicians, which was mostly violins and banjos. They had sawdust from the saw mill hauled up for to dance on. There were two areas. Each was big enough for about eight couples to dance. There was a young man dressed up, sitting on one of the stands. He was already drawing the bow on his violin. His hair was curly and a rich auburn red. Eight years later I married him.
>
> Everybody was having a lot of fun when two men got into a quarrel over a small girl who was dancing. She was about sixteen years old. From that the big fight started. There sure was a battle. Two men from Springfield almost got cut to pieces with knives. Everybody got to leaving. I'll never forget that dance. It was the thirty-first day of July, 1902. There was several got hurt in that fight. They had to be carried to the doctor's. The young man I mentioned playing the violin, put his violin under his arm and up that creek he went.

It is rare that a family has a wealth of written stories about their ancestors and the lives they lived. This would be a far less interesting and informative book without the stories by Annie Adcock. She left the following story about her life shortly after she met Gooden Adcock.

> When we moved to Sycamore Creek, I could read and write, as I had put one year up at Old Mt. Pleasant School. After we moved here, I learned very fast and finished the eighth grade, was starting in the ninth, when the Dillard family asked me to teach their little girls. Money was scarce, so I took the job of teaching Ruth and Cleo Dillard for five dollars a week. I bought myself some new clothes for I sure didn't have any.

We have been following the Riley Adcock branch of the family for some time now. It is important to include an event that occurred in the branch of Riley's brother, Anderson Adcock. As we wrote earlier, Anderson Adcock died in 1896. Living in the family home in 1900, were Anderson's widow, Caroline Smiley Adcock, his daughter, Callie, and his son, Taylor.

All of the various pieces of Anderson Adcock's land was purchased for one dollar by Taylor Adcock on January 26, 1907. Below is the transcript of the land transfer.

J.T. Pyles & et al. To, Taylor Adcock – Jan. 26th 1907.

For and in consideration of the sum of One Dollar cash in hand paid, the receipt of which is hereby acknowledged of Taylor Adcock, We, the Legal heirs and distributes of Anderson Adcock, deceased, have bargained and sold, to and by these presents do transfer and convey unto the said Taylor Adcock, his heirs and assigns, certain tracts or parcels of land in the 12th Civil District or Robertson County, State of Tennessee, as follows: to wit:

First, Beginning at a stake and pointers, formerly three red oaks but now down, on the south side of a ridge: thence North 80 poles, crossing Rules branch to a pile of rocks and pointers on a ridge, 25 poles on the North side of Rules branch; thence east 94 poles to a Sourwood; thence south crossing a branch in all 14 poles to a dead white oak, Acy Adcocks south west corner; thence east 106 poles to a gum and dogwood; thence South 66 poles to a chestnut and Spanish Oak on a ridge; thence North 89 ¼ deg. West 200 poles to the beginning, containing 100 acres more or less.

Second, Beginning at three red oaks, the corner of the first described tract above mentioned, thence North 62 poles to an Ash; thence west 52 poles to an Iron Wood on a branch; thence with its meanders in all 114 poles to a bush on the bank of said branch; thence south 20 ples to a white oak, Tate's corner; thence east with his line 156 poles to his corner, an oak and bush, thence to the beginning, containing **52 acres**, more or less, To have and to hold the said Tracts or parcels of land, with the appurtenances estate, title, and interest thereto belonging to the said Taylor Adcock, his heirs and assigns forever, and we do covenant and bind our heirs and representative to warrant and defend the title to our respective interest or shares in said lands above described to the said Taylor Adcock, his heirs and assigns, against the lawful claims of all persons whomsoever, In testimony whereof the said Taylor Adcock hereby agrees to take care of his mother during the remainder of her life.

Witness our hands this 26th day of January, 1907.

J.T. Pyles, M.E. Pyles, J.T. Greer, Tyler B. Greer, Elizabeth Tate, A.B. Adcock, Mattie Adcock, Jackey Adcock, N.F. Adcock, Dave S. Smiley, W.E. Tinnin, Hessie A. Tinnin, Martha Baxter, S.W. Baxter.

The people who signed over land formerly belonging to Anderson Adcock were:

J.T. Pyles and M.E. Pyles – James T. Pyles (1857-1936), and his wife, Mary Ellen Adcock Pyles (1860-1945), who was the daughter of Anderson Adcock.

J.T. Greer and Tyler B. Greer – This is James T. Greer (1861-1933), and his wife, Tyler B. Adcock Greer (1867-1939), who was the daughter of Anderson Adcock.

Elizabeth Tate – This is Anderson Adcock's daughter, Artemisa Elizabeth Adcock Tate (1850-1923). Her husband, Henry C. Tate, died in 1904.

A.B. Adcock and Mattie Adcock – Anderson B. Adcock (1882-1941), is the son of Sylvanus B. Adcock, and grandson of Anderson Adcock. A.B. Adcock's father, Sylvanus "Sill" Adcock died before 1907. Mattie Adcock (1883-1957) is Mattie Smiley Adcock, A.B. Adcock's wife.

Jackey Adcock – Jackey Lou Wilkerson Adcock (1861-1940) is the wife of Sylvanus B. Adcock, son of Anderson Adcock.

N. F. Adcock – Nick Franklin Adcock (1884-1963) is the son of Sylvanus B. Adcock and Jackey Lou Wilkerson Adcock.

Dave S. Smiley (1877-1924) Son of Dave Smiley and Mary Frances Adcock Smiley. He married Mary Elizabeth Adcock, daughter of Sylvanus "Sill" Adcock. She was Anderson Adcock's granddaughter.

W. E. Tinnin and Hessie A. Tinnin – This is William E. Tinnin (1842-1921) and his wife, Hessie Ann Adcock Tinnin (1852-1936), who is the daughter of Anderson Adcock.

Martha Baxter and S.W. Baxter – This is Martha Jane Adcock Baxter (1854-1931), daughter of Anderson Adcock, and her husband, Samuel W. Baxter (1847-1927).

This accounts for all of Anderson Adcock's children except, Callie, who was living at home with her mother, Caroline Smiley Adcock, and her brother, Taylor Adcock. Anderson Adcock's daughters, Talitha Adcock (1869-1887) and Eveline "Eva" Adcock Greer (1859-1888), were already deceased.

We included this land transfer because it will help the reader understand why certain members of the family are buried at the Adcock Cemetery (Anderson Adcock Cemetery) which is located on a portion of the land transferred to Taylor Adcock in 1907.

On September 19, 1909, Riley's wife, Mary Frances Smiley Adcock, died. She is buried at Forest Grove Cemetery in Joelton, Tennessee.

In late spring, on April 10, 1910, at her parents' home, Annie Biggs married Gooden Adcock. Besides the immediate family, Tom Smiley, who was Gooden's cousin was there. Annie's brother, Jack Biggs, went to Joelton, in his buggy, and got the Reverend George Milliken, a Baptist preacher, to perform the ceremony.

After the wedding, there was a nice supper consisting of chicken and dumplings, turnip greens, and potato salad. There was plenty of coffee, cornbread & biscuits. The Reverend George Milliken ate supper with the family. Gooden and Annie went to his father's home and made it their home for about three and a half years. Living in the house was Gooden's father, Riley Adcock, and his brother,

Dave Adcock. Gooden's mother had been dead for about a year.

Riley Adcock did the cooking because, Annie did not know how to cook. She soon learned. Annie and Gooden enjoyed fishing in Sycamore Creek.

While living with Riley Adcock, Gooden and Annie had two daughters. Myrtle was born on July 11, 1911. Clara was born on November 15, 1913. In May, 1914, Gooden and Annie moved to a house on a farm along Sycamore Creek that Gooden had purchased. Gooden would get one daughter on each knee and rock them every evening.

Morris Riley "Gooden" Adcock with his wife, Annie Biggs Adcock,
with their daughters, Myrtle (standing) and Clara (in Annie's lap)

It wasn't long until Gooden's father, Riley, moved in with them. Annie was surprised that Riley had decided to move in with them. She wrote the following about it.

> Well, we was surprised when Grandpa took his bed down and moved in with us. He had a little red mule he called Mike. He rode this little mule wherever he went, sometimes with Myrtle in his arms.

> Myrtle and Clara followed the old man and their Daddy to feed hogs and mules every night. One evening Clara lay down by her Daddy while he was shucking corn. He threw shucks all

over her. She had gone to sleep. He got through shucking and thought she went to the house.

I looked and saw my husband coming. He had Myrtle, but I didn't see Clara. I hollered and asked where she was. Her Daddy said he thought she had come to the house. The creek ran along by the barn where they were feeding, so it scared me into a fit. We looked everywhere. He was scared stiff. Finally, he said he'd look in the corncrib one more time. When he did, Clara woke up and raised up out of the shucks. He said he was going to whip her, but I was so glad we found her, I run with her to the house.

Grandpa Adcock would get up and go back to his old house every day and work in his blacksmith shop. He told me one time, he heard the ghost of his wife in the old house, which was up on a hill from the blacksmith shop. He said she would walk from the table to the stove. He would listen at eleven o'clock every day, for she would come on the porch and call him for dinner. He said he would sometimes walk up under a big apple tree which wasn't far from the house. There he said, he couldn't hear her anymore.

We lived on the creek. We hunted in the woods. At that time we never had any extra furniture. Nothing more than we had to have to use. We had no means of travel other than a two-horse wagon and two mules. The creek was between us and everyone who lived around. When it got up, there was no getting anywhere.

It was in the days of the coal-oil lamp. If the creek got out of the banks and the oil got low, that meant no light. If the matches gave out there was no fire until the old man got out his musket and loaded it with powder and cap, with cotton in the end of the barrel. He shot it and then picked up the cotton and blew on it to start a fire. Those were the happiest days of our lives.

One family gave a Square Dance. Most had been invited, but, some boys were left out. This was meant as a slight. While all were in the house having fun with music and laughter, these boys slipped up to the old man's hen house and plucked every feather off his chickens. Since it was cold weather, the man and his wife had to make clothes for the chickens to keep them from freezing till new feathers grew. Music was by Dave Adcock on banjo, my husband on fiddle and Dan Raymer on guitar.

Annie could read and write, and had even taught others how to do the same. But, Gooden never learned to read or write. Annie explained why. It also verifies the existence of that one-room log schoolhouse on the Forest Grove Cemetery property.

Around 1886, Gooden attended a one-room school that was around the location of Forest Grove Cemetery. On his first day, one of the Baxter boys pushed his head in the spring. Riley went home and never went back to school.

Two months after Annie and Gooden moved with their two young daughters, Riley Adcock became ill. He was taken to a hospital run by Dr. Lang, at Joelton. Dr. Lang had come from Lansing, Michigan, and opened a hospital where the funeral home now stands. Riley Adcock stayed in the hospital for about six weeks in the summer of 1914. He stayed out in a tent as the house was full. He got better and Gooden went after him in an old buggy. That was about the time Ernest Earl Adcock was born. Gooden's and Annie's first son, Ernest, was born on July 17, 1914.

When Ernest was small, Gooden and Annie moved across Sycamore Creek to another house. Riley still lived with them. He still went back to his old home place every day and worked in his blacksmith shop. Gooden's and Annie's daughter, Ruby Frances Adcock, was born on February 23, 1918. Their son, Morris Riley Adcock, III, known as Morris, was born on March 15, 1919.

Eight days later, Gooden's brother, Dave, went to check on his father at the blacksmith shop. He found Riley laying on the floor, unable to move. He had a stroke. Dave ran and got Gooden. Annie couldn't leave because of the baby, Morris. So, she sent little Myrtle, who was eight, and Clara, who was six, to the nearest telephone to call a doctor. Gooden and Dave moved their father to the old house. He died soon after.

Riley Adcock died on March 23, 1919. He is buried at Forest Grove Cemetery in Joelton, next to his wife. For that branch of the Adcock family, the next generation would have to carry on.

# Chapter Nine

## Brighter Days Ahead

### (1920 - 1929)

When Riley Adcock died, his sons, Gooden and Dave washed him and dressed him. There was no funeral home in the area in those days. Riley had always carried his money in his pocket. There were also no banks in the area. His sons found that he had a large sum of money on him when he died. Gooden suggested they put the money in an old shoe and throw it up in the closet where no one would think to look for it.

"Blacksmith Shop" oil painting by Samuel S. Carr would have been
similar to the blacksmith shop of Riley Adcock

After the funeral, Dave went back to the old house by the creek. Dave was a fifty-year-old bachelor. He had several lady friends, but, somehow he decided he didn't want a life-time partner. It was at least a half a mile to anyone's home from where he lived alone. Annie described what happened next.

It was talked far and near that Dave was loaded with money since his daddy died. One Friday night in July, about nine o'clock, Dave was closed up in the old three-room house.

He had the windows nailed up half way. It was hard to see inside. He heard someone call him from the outside. He finally answered the call, and they told him they wanted to go hunting with him. He told them he did not want to go hunting, so they went on.

Sunday afternoon they caught him away from the house, coming in. He stopped by the end of the house to feed an old rooster he had in a coop. He had his gun in his hand, but when he raised up he saw two pistols pointed in his face. They told him to throw up his hands or take his medicine. Of course, he had no other choice.

They marched him inside the house, made him lay down on the bed, where they tied him with bed sheets. One stood guard over him while the other one raided the house. The first place they looked was in the closet. That old shoe was the first thing they looked for, and they got it. They also raided the whole house. When they started to leave they told him, if he got loose before twelve o'clock, they would still be around and they'd shoot him.

So, he lay there most of the night. He came up to the house next morning and told us, but told us not to tell no one or they'd come back again. I told him that's what the law is for, to catch thieves. So, I went and called the law. They come and they laid it on two boys, who they put in the penitentiary for a long period of time. But, I never believed those two boys done the bad deed.

There was two men who everybody knew. Some had seen them come back this road that leads to Dave Adcock's house. I am perfectly satisfied it was them, and not the two boys, who should have taken the blame and put up the time. I wouldn't even go to the trial because I didn't think it was them.

After a good many years, the father of one of those boys came to see my husband and his brother Dave. He asked them to sign a paper to let his boys out. My husband brought the paper to the house and asked me, if I was in his place, would I sign it? I told him I would, since I never believed it was them to start with. So, he did. And, one day I met one of these boys at the market on the Public Square in Nashville. He told me he had been dirty, but, he did not rob Dave Adcock.

In late 1919, Gooden and Annie, and their children, moved from their house on Sycamore Creek, to a house on Springfield Road, now Whites Creek Pike. Gooden had done well. Some of this can be attributed to the paved road between Nashville and Springfield, which reduced the time and cost of getting farm goods to market. Cash crops could be sold in Springfield. Produce such as vegetables and eggs, could be sold in Nashville at the market on the Public Square.

With increasing populations in Nashville and Springfield, demand for timber increased. People were also demanding more farm produce. There was a high demand for products like tobacco, chickens and pigs. Gooden's farm was profitable. He was able to provide nice things for his children. He even purchased an automobile for Annie. It was a 1919 Overland 90 Touring Car, and the first car on the Ridge, according to Annie.

1919 Overland 90 Touring Car

Annie drove very well. She took Myrtle and Clara to school. Forest Grove School was located across from Bethel Church of Christ on what is now Whites Creek Pike. It was a white frame two-room schoolhouse with a lunch room. The toilet was separate and behind the school.

Annie holding Morris in 1920. Ruby is sitting in chair.

Ernest Adcock about 1920

Prohibition began on January 16, 1920, when the Eighteenth Amendment went into effect. The Nineteenth amendment to the United States Constitution, ratified on August 18, 1920, granted women the right to vote. The lives of Gooden and Annie were bright. There seemed to be an optimism across the whole country.

In 1921, Gooden and Annie had their sixth child, a baby girl they named Hazel Lorene Adcock. They called her Rene. She was born on May 25, 1921. Their son, Millard Carroll Adcock, followed. Millard was born on February 16, 1924.

The whole family was shocked when, Gooden's brother, Dave Adcock, took sick. He was still living in the old house by Sycamore Creek. Dr. Dozer attended him for two days. He died of Typhoid Fever on August 15, 1924. He was only fifty-five years old. He was buried at Forest Grove Cemetery.

On March 8, 1925, Gooden and Annie had another son. They named him Roy Wallace Adcock. This was a golden time. Radio was becoming popular. WSM radio, in Nashville, began broadcasting a one-hour show called "The WSM Barn Dance" on November 28, 1925. It was hosted by George D. Hay. This was the beginning of the Grand Ole Opry.

The decade was full of exciting news. King Tut's Tomb was discovered in 1921, in the Valley of the Kings, in Egypt. The first Macy's Thanksgiving Day parade took place in New York, in 1924. On May 5, 1925, Tennessee school teacher, John Scopes, was arrested for teaching the theory of evolution. In 1927, Charles Lindbergh, made the first nonstop transatlantic flight in his plane, "The Spirit of St. Louis." In 1929, penicillin is first used to fight infection.

Gooden and Annie welcomed a new daughter, Norma Jean Adcock. She was born on June 15, 1928. It was a happy time for the family. But, the decade did not end well. On July 3, 1929, Collins Adcock, son of Carter Adcock, and Gooden's uncle, died of "infirmatives of age." He left behind his wife, Alice, and his children; Vernon, Lum, Mary, and Obie. He was buried at the cemetery at the old Walker Place.

Three months later the stock market crashed. It occurred on October 24, 1929, and was called "Black Thursday." U.S. Securities lost $26 billion dollars. It was the first event of what would become the Great Depression. No group was harder hit than farmers. Farm income across the nation fell by a staggering two-thirds during the Depression's first three years.

The Great Depression was just the beginning of the many challenges Gooden and Annie would face in the coming days.

# Chapter Ten

## Darker Days

(1930 - 1941)

Gooden was feeling the pressures of falling prices for farm products and the creeping effects of the Great Depression. It had grown more difficult to meet expenses. A while earlier, he had made a decision that proved to be unwise.

Some of the local farmers were finding it profitable to market their moonshine in Nashville. They had made moonshine for years for their own use. Now, under Prohibition, there was a large demand for illegal spirits.

Gooden, and a friend of his, were tempted to get in on the money-making opportunity. Unknown to Annie, Gooden, and his friend, Marshall, had been operating a still deep in the woods. Revenue Agents were on the lookout for rising smoke, which would reveal the presence of an operating still. It was easy to spot that smoke on the clear cold days of January.

One day, Gooden and his friend saw a trail of dust as a car sped back the road toward their still. Before they could douse the fire and escape, two revenue agents appeared and arrested Gooden and his friend. They were taken to jail in Springfield.

On January 10, Gooden was in Circuit Court in Springfield. He agreed to plead guilty to the charge of manufacturing liquor. The trial occurred on October 14, 1930. Gooden was found guilty. He was sentenced to ninety days in jail and fined $250, plus court costs. We don't know when Gooden was released. We do know the fine and court costs amounted to $313.54. A record from the county workhouse shows he paid the court costs.

Gooden and Annie certainly felt the pressure of the pending trial when their son, Billy Garner Adcock, was born on August 4, 1930.

Myrtle Adcock's daughter wrote that her mama and daddy were married on December 28, 1930, in Ashland City, on a side porch of a preacher's house. When Myrtle and Earl Harris were first going out together, he lived in the Shay House. It was a nice brick home. They had a piano. Myrtle's sister, Clara, would play the piano and Earl would sing. Myrtle and Earl would sometimes go out with Clara, and her future husband, Alvin Coles. Just before Myrtle and Earl married, the stock market crashed. Earl's family lost everything and had to move.

1930 had brought a dizzying series of events to the family, some good and some bad. The effects of the economy still weighed heavily on them. The consequences of Gooden's failed attempt at moonshining added to their woes. That unhappiness would pale by comparison to what happened next.

On Wednesday, May 13, 1931, the older boys were riding back from the fields. It was a typical day. Morris, who was eleven years old, slipped off the mule he was riding and caught his foot in the harness. The mule became frightened and began to run. Ernest and Millard chased after the runaway mule for more than a mile. When they finally stopped the mule, Morris was dead.

Morris' funeral was held at Forest Grove Methodist Church. He was buried in the cemetery across the road.

Morris Riley Adcock (1919 – 1931)

The family was still in grief when, suddenly, their house caught on fire. There was no fire department in that part of the country. There was nothing they could do but watch, while the pretty little white frame house, and all of its contents, were destroyed by the fire. There was no homeowners insurance for the average farmer. Gooden and Annie lost everything except the piano and library table. They were grateful for that.

They moved into a smaller house a short distance down the road. It was at the location of the present house of their granddaughter, Bess Ann Sircy, on Whites Creek Pike. Neighbors pitched in and helped as they could. Someone gave a small puppy to the children to cheer them. It was a difficult time for all of them.

People have often said bad things happen in threes. This was certainly true for Gooden and Annie, and their children. Not long after they settled into the little house, a dog ran into the Adcock's yard and attacked their puppy. The following story ran in a Nashville newspaper on July 30, 1931.

## Imperiled Lives for Wounded Puppy

—Staff Photo.

Incurring risk of death in its most horrible form, these children dressed the hurts of their pet puppy when the little animal was almost torn to pieces by a rabid German police dog, nursing and cuddling the poor sufferer with a tenderness and devotion that would not have faltered had they realized the danger themselves.

When it was established that the big dog had hydrophobia, Dr. J. J. Lentz, county health officer, decreed that the children must take the Pasteur prophylactic without delay, as the slightest abrasion of the skin coming in contact with saliva of a mad dog, admits the deadly germs to the human life blood.

These "volunteer nurses" are the children of Mr. and Mrs. M. R. Adcock of the Forest Grove community, four miles north of Joelton. In the picture are from left to right Jean, 3, with her doll that has made each trip; Lorene, 10; Ruby, 11, with Baby Billy, 11 months, who was too sleepy to pose for a photograph, but who had caressed the puppy, intuitively divining something was wrong; Roy, 6, and Mildred, 7. Another brother, Ernest, 7, is taking the anti-rabies treatment also.

The caption under the photograph tells what happened after the dog attacked the puppy. It reads:

Incurring risk of death in its most horrible form, these children dressed the hurts of their pet puppy when the little animal was almost torn to pieces by a rabid German police dog, nursing and cuddling the poor sufferer with a tenderness and devotion that would not have faltered had they realized the danger themselves.

When it was established that the big dog had hydrophobia, Dr. J.J. Lentz, county health officer, decreed that the children must take the Pasteur prophylactic without delay, as the slightest abrasion of the skin coming in contact with saliva of a mad dog, admits the deadly germs to the human life blood.

These "volunteer nurses" are the children of Mr. and Mrs. M. R. Adcock of the Forest Grove community, four miles north of Joelton.

In the picture are from left to right: Jean, 3, with her doll that has made each trip; Lorene, 10; Ruby, 13, with baby Billy, 11 months old, who was too sleepy to pose for a photograph, but who had caressed the puppy, intuitively divining something was wrong; Roy, 6, and Millard, 7. Another brother, Ernest, 7, is taking the anti-rabies treatment also.

*Note: The newspaper article listed Ernest as age 7. He was actually 17.*

1931 had been an unbearable year for the family. As any farmer will tell you, some years are just bad. All one can do is keep their faith and hope that the next year is better. Things did seem to get better. On January 17, 1932, their first grandchild was born. Helen Juanita Harris was the daughter of their oldest daughter, Myrtle, and her husband Earl Harris. On October 14, 1932, their daughter, Betty Lou Adcock was born.

Annie, who had nine children to raise, decided her best plan was to move to Nashville, and find a paying job. Her children living with her, ranged in age. The oldest daughter still living at home was Clara, who was twenty. The youngest child was Betty, who was less than one year old.

Annie found a house at 840 Scott Avenue, in North Nashville. She soon had a job selling candy and apples in the Stahlman Building in downtown Nashville. The Stahlman Building was a twelve-story office building on the southwest corner of Third Avenue North and Union Street. The Forth National Bank was on the first floor.

A few weeks after Annie moved to Nashville, Gooden joined her. The Great Depression had taken a solid hold on the economy. The Works Progress Administration, part of Franklin Roosevelt's "New Deal," put many people to work. Gooden found such a job at Centennial Park, on West End Avenue, in Nashville. The WPA project there was to build a swimming pool and bath house. It was a one-story, H-shaped building, with a red tile roof. That project started in 1933.

Annie had the older girls to help with the other children. Clara, who was twenty, took a job at Werthan Bag Company, but she helped when she could. Ruby, who was fifteen, looked after the smallest children; Jean, age five, Billy, age three, and Betty, almost a year old. The other children were in school. They attended Fehr Elementary School on Fifth Avenue North. Rene, who was twelve, and Millard, who was nine, probably enjoyed the school, although they never mentioned it as adults. Roy, on the other hand, when he was an adult, told his daughter, Carolyn, that he enjoyed Fehr Elementary School. He also mentioned that he often played at Sulphur Dell, which was a professional baseball field located not far from their house.

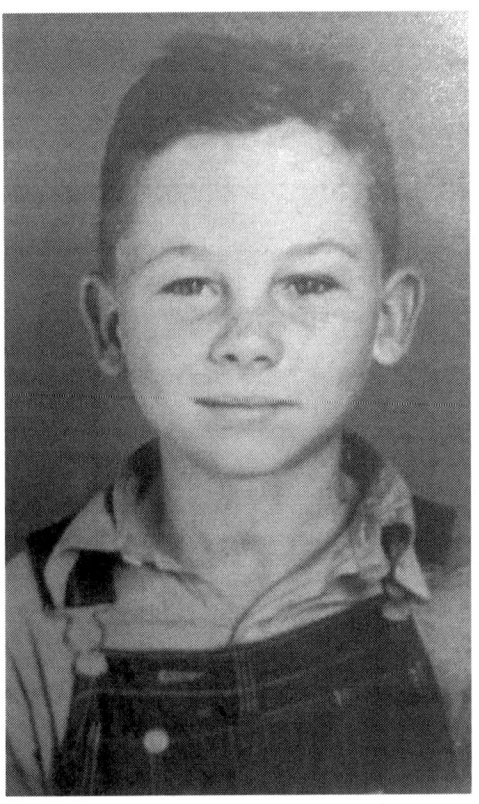

Roy Adcock

Annie lost one of her most capable helpers in the summer of 1933. Her daughter, Clara, married Jesse Alvin Coles, on July 8, 1933, in Franklin, Kentucky.

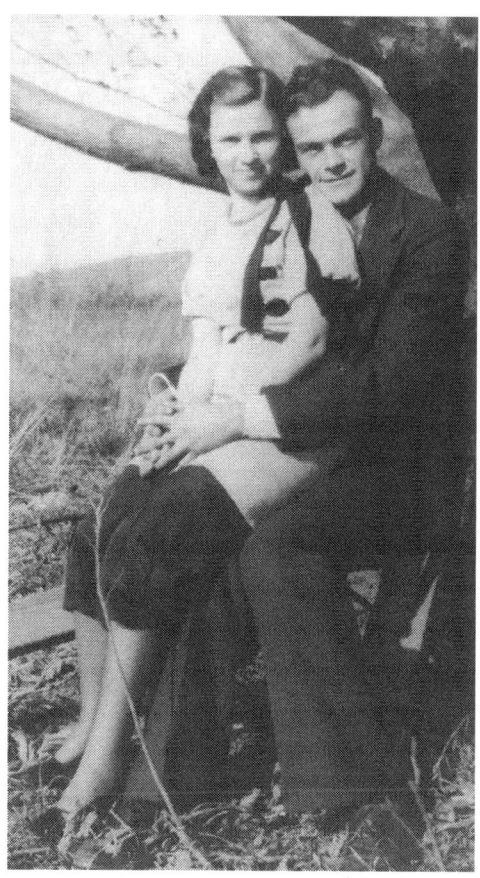

Clara and Alvin Coles in 1933

The family lived in a section of North Nashville known as "Cab Hollow." It was a working class neighborhood. It got its name from some early textile mill workers who came to the area from DeKalb County, Tennessee, in the late 1800s. Over the years, the early "DeKalb Hollow" became simplified to "Cab Hollow."

In 1935, the family moved from Nashville, to Union Hill, Tennessee. Union Hill is near Greenbrier and about eight miles northeast of the Forest Grove community. The school-age children of Gooden and Annie Adcock went to Union Hill School. Union Hill School was built around 1908.

Union Hill School photograph from 1935. Identified are; Jean Adcock, first row, 4th from left; Roy Adcock, first row 7th from the left; and, Rene Adcock, fourth row, 3rd from left.

Ernest Adcock was already out of school, but one of the young students at Union Hill School caught his attention. Annie Marshall Binkley and her family lived on Ivy Point Road. The Binkley family attended Ivy Point Church of Christ. Ernest asked Annie Marshall's father if he could date her. Annie Marshall's father told Ernest that he could, if he went to church with her. Ernest started attending, and soon joined the congregation.

Like most Union Hill School students, Annie Marshall walked to school. On September 8, 1936, Annie Marshall walked to school as usual. Only this time, she stopped at Galbreath's Store where Ernest was waiting for her. They went to the courthouse in Gallatin, Tennessee, and were married that day.

Gooden's and Annie's daughter, Ruby Adcock married George Patterson on March 2, 1936.

Newly-Weds, Ruby and George Patterson with Earl and Myrtle Harris

In 1938, the family returned to the Forest Grove community. They moved to a house on the corner of Springfield Pike and Coopertown Road. The children who were at home, and old enough, went to Forest Grove School. This included Millard, Jean, Roy and Billy. The old white frame school was still in use, but a new brick school was being built.

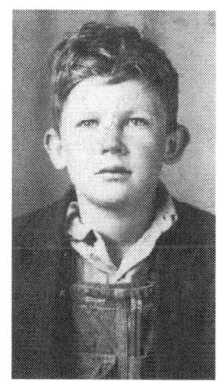

Jean Adcock and Millard Adcock and Bill Adcock about 1938

In 1939, Betty, who was seven, started at Forest Grove School. She said her mother wouldn't let her go to school until she was seven, because she was so small.

The decade of the 1930s, was nearing the end. Things were much improved from those first few years at the beginning of the decade. But, things have a way of changing in an instant.

On June 17, 1939, Gooden's brother, Will Adcock, was found dead in the Sycamore Creek bottoms. He had been shot. The shooting was listed as a homicide, but no one ever knew what happened. Will was buried at Forest Grove Cemetery.

Shortly after Will's death, his wife, Laura Chambliss Adcock, sold the property to Gooden. She moved to Nashville with her son, Obie Adcock. At that time, the road that led from Springfield Pike back to Sycamore Creek was a small dirt road that ran beside the home of Mrs. Mattie Lane.

In 1941, Gooden and Annie moved to the house back that small dirt road. With them were their children; Millard, Roy, Jean, Billy, and Betty. After that, things settled down a bit for the family. The boys were old enough to be useful in the fields. Gooden raised tobacco as a cash crop. There were fields of corn of several varieties. Annie's garden took shape and produced an abundance of vegetables. An apple orchard, across the road from the house, yielded a large harvest in the fall. The creek bottoms were planted in beans. Blackberries and strawberries grew wild and plentiful.

# Chapter Eleven

## The War Years and After

### (1941-1953)

World War II was on everyone's minds. The United States had managed to avoid direct engagement in the conflict that was quickly spreading around the world. That changed. On December 7, 1941, the Japanese attacked the United States Naval Base at Pearl Harbor, in Hawaii. President Roosevelt came on the radio with a somber announcement. At the close of his radio address to the nation, he said, "With confidence in our armed forces - with the unbounding determination of our people - we will gain the inevitable triumph - so help us God.

I ask that the Congress declare that since the unprovoked and dastardly attack by Japan on Sunday, December 7, a state of war has existed between the United States and the Japanese empire." The United State was now officially engaged in World War II.

Jean Adcock, who was thirteen, was focused on a more pleasant event. The new brick schoolhouse that replaced the aging white frame building had been completed. Dedication of the new Forest Grove School was scheduled for December 7, 1941. She described the day, which was clearly etched in her memory.

> I got dressed up, put on my "beanie", a felt hat with a long feather on it, and I walked up to the school to the dedication. It was on a Sunday afternoon. We had been going to school in the old white frame building that stood over by the side of the new one facing the road.

> The old school had a potbellied stove at the rear of the room, which would get so hot that it would catch the wall on fire. The kids didn't wait to march out orderly, but dove out the windows.

> Getting back to the dedication. About half way through the ceremony, someone came in with the news that Japan had attacked Pearl Harbor. At that time, I didn't know where Pearl Harbor was located, but I knew that the news was bad. They stopped the dedication ceremony and we all listened to the radio as President F.D.R. declared war on Japan.

> I went home and told the folks that the United States was at war with Japan. They didn't believe me. We had no radio or paper at that time. However, it didn't take long before more news was heard about it from the War Department, calling up our boys to fight for their country. It didn't take much coaxing because everyone was "fighting mad" at the Japs for attacking Pearl Harbor. It just about destroyed our Navy.

Life in the United States changed dramatically. Defense jobs became available. Manufacturing of automobiles stopped and those plants shifted to building tanks and airplanes. Rationing of gasoline, tires, and other goods affected everyone. Perhaps, not everyone. Some things go on as normal, even in the most difficult of times. One example was the 4H Club's First Prize won by Roy Adcock for his beans.

Roy Adcock won 1st prize at 4H Club for his beans in 1941

A couple of years into the war, people were looking for something cheerful to take their minds off of the news they were hearing on the radio. Ruby noticed that her sister, Jean, was looking a little sad. Jean moved on to Joelton High School. Ruby suggested that they get permission from the school to hold a dance. Jean told the story.

> Ruby had a record player and some good records. We got permission to hold the dance at the school. My brother, Millard, played the records and kept the music going. There was a big crowd there and we danced the Virginia reel, and other square dances. Mr. Charlie Sterry commented about how well I danced, and said that I looked a lot like Annie, my mother, when she was my age. A swell time was had by all. I know that I enjoyed it.

Joelton High School – Jean Adcock is second from right on first row, in white sweater

In the summer of 1943, Alvin Coles, husband of Clara Adcock Coles, took a job at Oak Ridge. It was a part of the war effort. Oak Ridge was established in 1942, as a production site for the Manhattan Project, the massive operation that developed the atomic bomb.

Photo Badge that allowed Alvin entrance to the Oak Ridge facility

Alvin worked for a contractor who ran pipes for the site. He moved into a boarding house in Clinton, Tennessee, but soon bought a trailer so his wife, and young son, could join him. In a letter to Clara, on August 5, 1943, he wrote the following:

Hello Sweetheart,

How are my two babies tonight? I'm still feeling pretty well except for a cold.

Well darling, I got the trailer yesterday evening late but I couldn't get them to move it for me until today. I had it moved to the Knoxville trailer camp. It's about half way between Clinton and Knoxville.

I believe you are really going to like the home I've got for you now. It sure is nice. Not new by a long way, but it's all steel and has a good cook stove, two beds, sink, cabinets, closets and all of the wood work is mahogany.

I have about run myself to death trying to get everything arranged and trying to work, too, ten hours a day.

My gas tickets are not so many. I put in an application today for a C gas book out on the job and I'm supposed to get it tomorrow. At least I hope I do.

Be a sweet girl.

Alvin

Note: The "C gas book" he mentioned meant he would be able to buy more gasoline. Due to war time shortages, gas rationing became the law in 1942. Every motorist was issued a windshield sticker displaying a letter. "A" for most motorists, allowed 3 gallons per week. "B" was for war workers and allowed 8 gallons per week. "C" was for people deemed essential to the war effort. It allowed unlimited gas purchases. Gas rationing continued until August 15, 1945.

Alvin and Clara were not the only ones who moved their family to support the war effort. George Patterson, and his wife, Ruby Adcock Patterson, moved to Detroit, Michigan. George's and Ruby's daughter, Bess Ann, recalls the time their family spent in Detroit, during World War II:

We were living at 5617 Linwood Ave, in Detroit. We were up there because daddy was in service, and worked where they made guns and ammunition for the federal government. He worked as a military guard (M.P.).

We lived in an apartment building on the second floor. Uncle Erick's parents lived downstairs. Uncle Erick stayed with them. He was in the Army, and came home a lot, he must have been stationed close by at the time.

We had to keep the lights out during the day to save electricity. Everything was rationed during that time. The apartments were dark during the day because there were not many windows. Ma Hansen used a carpet sweeper to clean the carpet in their house. She used coffee grounds because she said it cleaned and killed the dust. I will never forget that!

Aunt Jean came up to visit a few times and Uncle Erick just fell for her right off. She was still in school but she fell for him also! She would come up to Detroit, when she could. He started coming down to Joelton, for two or three years. Then, they decided to get married. She dropped out of high school, they got married, and they moved to Michigan. She finished school after her children were born.

My sister, Reba, and I could sometimes go downstairs and sit on the stoop with Pa Hansen to get fresh air and see the sunshine. He was a lot of fun, and Ma Hansen was a clown. We loved to visit them.

Reba was about three years old, and I was about five, when we lived in Detroit. Daddy had to work a lot. Sometimes days at a time. Uncle Millard, Uncle Roy and Aunt Rene always seemed to be around. We had to stay in the house. We were not allowed outside. Only the men were allowed to go to store and other places.

They were having race riots, and the Army trucks rode the streets all day long, and all night. The trucks were loaded with soldiers with guns loaded and bayonets on them! They were in full military gear! We had a big bay window that looked out over the street. We would sit in the window and watch the trucks, loaded with soldiers, ride up and down the street.

There was a curfew. That is about all I remember about that.

NOTE: The race riot in Detroit, occurred from June 20 to 22, 1943.

From *Life* magazine, published on July 5, 1943: "White and black Detroiters slugged, clubbed, gouged, stoned, kicked, stabbed and shot each other until 31 were dead, more than 600 injured and 1,800 arrested. After several thousand soldiers in full battle dress put down the riot, a fact-finding committee appointed by Governor Kelly of Michigan went to work to determine its causes."

My sister, Elaine, was born in 1944. Daddy was able to get out of service soon after Elaine was released from the doctor. We caught the L&N train to Nashville, and arrived at Union Station. The first place we went was to Joelton, to see Mammy and Pappy Adcock and the rest of the family!

As we learned from Ruby's daughter, Jean Adcock met her future husband, Erick Hansen, during World War II. Jean's daughter, Carol, recalled how her parents met.

When Ruby and George Patterson were living in Detroit, they lived next to Dad and his family. Mom went to visit her sister, Ruby, when she was fifteen, and while there, met Dad. Dad took her and his mother for a steak dinner. Standing on their front porch, looking across the yard at Mom, Dad told his mother, "I'm going to marry that girl one day." Such a hoot!

He was just shy of ten years older than Mom. He came to Tennessee, to visit, and stayed at her parent's house, I think. I'm not sure how many times he actually came down to Tennessee, before he went into the Army. Most of their courtship consisted of letter writing while he was in the Army.

Dad enlisted later than his friends, because, when most of his buddies were signing up, he felt obligated to stay at home to help his parents. He gave them part of his paycheck each payday to help run the household, as did Uncle Carl, because their Mom didn't work outside the home, and their Dad worked general labor jobs, which probably didn't pay well.

Dad was in Europe during WWII, but he never talked about his service, which I've learned was very common with most of those WWII vets. They must have seen some horrible things that no one should be witness to. Dad's father, Aage Hansen, died while Dad was in Europe.

Erick Hanson served with the US Army, 71st Division in World War II

He came home in June, 1946, and started looking for a job so he'd have the money to drive down to visit Mom. By the time he'd earned enough money, the weather had started getting bad in Michigan, so he tried a couple of times to make it down for a visit before he finally was able to make it. There was no such things as interstates, so the roads he had to travel were probably in pretty bad shape after a snow storm.

He and Mom had been writing about getting married. Mom was a senior at Joelton High School, and her parents wanted her to finish. Dad, however, asked her to marry him and she said yes, because she wanted Dad more than she wanted to finish high school, so love won out! She did go back when my sister, Linda, and I were in high school, and finished getting her high school diploma. I wish Dad hadn't been so set on her not working, because I believe she would have excelled in college and could have gone on to do no telling what! She was a smart little lady! They got married on December 28, 1946, and moved up to Michigan.

A newspaper announcement in Nashville, described the wedding and reception that followed.

"One of the outstanding weddings of the fall season was the marriage of Miss Jean Adcock of Joelton to Erick Hanson which was solemnized recently at the Girls Home of the Central Church of Christ, with A. R. Holton officiating. Mrs. Roy Adcock served as the bride's attendant and Roy Adcock served as best man. Following the ceremony, Mr. and Mrs. Morris Adcock entertained at a dinner at their home at Joelton. For the occasion fall flowers were used throughout the home."

Jean's sister, Rene, joined the WAVES (Women Accepted for Volunteer Emergency Services) on May 29, 1945. She was assigned to the Hospital Corps. Because of the war, and a rapidly growing need for trained medical personnel, a Hospital Corps training facility was opened at the Naval Hospital in Brooklyn, New York. That is where Rene went to school. In a letter Rene wrote to her sister, Clara, on September 5, 1945, she wrote:

> Dear Clara and Alvin and kids. Sorry I haven't written in so long, but I'm going to school and these studies are plenty tough. I have to keep my mind on them and really study. We have exams every week, so you see, they keep me plenty busy.
>
> I'm sending you a picture. Hope you like it. Tell everyone hello for me and write to me real soon.
>
> Love to all, Rene

The photograph Rene sent with the letter to her sister, Clara

While in service, Rene met her future husband, a young Navy fellow named Pearly Marvin Frazier. He had enlisted on March 25, 1942. Boats served in World War II and the Korean War.

Rene and "Boats" Frazier

World War II ended when the Japanese surrendered, unconditionally, on September 2, 1945. Two months later, Roy Adcock married Dorothy Virginia Maynard. Everyone called her Dot. They were married on November 5, 1945, in Bowling Green, Kentucky.

Roy Adcock and Dorothy "Dot" Maynard

Roy met Dot at Morgan Park in North Nashville. Morgan Park was close to Sulfur Dell Ball Park and was next to Ferh School. There were movies shown in the park every Tuesday and Thursday night. The movie playing the night they met was "Song of the South."

Dorothy Maynard's family lived on Delta Avenue, a few block away from Roy's older sister, Ruby and her husband, George Patterson. Ruby and George had moved, with their three daughters, from Detroit, to Nashville, in 1944. Roy was staying with them.

Dot was a straight "A" student in the tenth grade at Hume Fogg High School. The school was located in downtown Nashville. Dot rode the bus to school. Just across the street, on 7th Avenue, was a printing company, where Roy worked. Roy watched out the window every day to see Dot get off the bus. When she did, they waved at each other.

On November 4th, they made plans to elope the next day. Roy was to meet Dot at her bus stop the next morning. When she got to the bus stop, Roy was waiting for her. Ruby and George were waiting in their car, along with Roy's brother, Millard, and two friends, Pete Russell and Dorothy Swindle. They drove to Bowling Green, Kentucky, for the wedding.

After getting their blood test and license, they went to the preacher's house. Because Dot was only sixteen, the preacher asked who would sign for her. Ruby, thinking quickly, told the preacher that she was Dot's mother. The preacher seemed hesitant. Ruby leaned over and whispered to him that Dot was pregnant. She wasn't, but Ruby's story satisfied the preacher and he married Roy and Dot.

Dot sent a telegram to her father from Bowling Green, telling him that she and Roy had gotten married. They all arrived back at Ruby's and George's house about 11:30 that night. Roy and Dot spent their wedding night there. The next morning, Roy and Dot went to her parent's house. Dot's parents were okay with the marriage. Roy and Dot moved in with them for a while.

They eventually rented a house on Delta Avenue. That's where they lived when their children, Steve, Sue, and Carolyn were born. They moved to a house on Whites Creek Pike, in Joelton, before Roy Jr. was born, in 1953.

Meanwhile, Ernest and Annie moved into the old house on Sycamore Creek. It was the same house his mother, Annie Biggs Adcock had moved into in 1901, when she and her family left Cheatham County. It was the same house that would be occupied by his sister, Ruby, and her husband George, after they moved back to the Joelton area from Nashville.

Ernest had worked for the railroad. He and another man were in the engine of a passenger train when they looked ahead and saw another train heading toward them on the same track. They managed to switch to a siding just in time to avoid a head-on collision. Ernest quit the railroad at that point.

Ernest and Annie Marshall Adcock with six of their children around 1947

Myrtle Adcock Harris took her eleven-year-old daughter, Earlene, to Nashville in December, 1948, so she could sing on the radio with four of her friends. The show was the popular WSM radio Gospel music program, Wally Fowler's *All Night Sing*, broadcast from the Ryman Auditorium. At 11:00 pm, Wally Fowler brought Earlene and her friends on to sing some Christmas songs. At the end of the show, Earlene returned to sing with the entire cast.

When Annie Biggs Adcock's half-brother, Doll Biggs died, on May 26, 1949, Earlene and her sister, Juanita, sang at the funeral service. She recalled she was scared because her sister made her stand next to the casket. They sang again at the burial at Forest Grove Cemetery. These experiences gave Earlene a life-long love of Gospel music. She continues to sing Gospel songs.

In March, 1951, Billy Garner Adcock, joined the Army. He enlisted in Nashville, and took basic training at Fort Benning, Georgia. His parents, Gooden and Annie, rode with his sister, Jean, and her husband Erick, to see him while he was stationed at Fort Benning. They brought Billy a freshly baked cake. Along the way, Erick had to slam on the brakes. Everyone was shaken by the sudden stop. Annie looked down and saw that her feet had come down on the cake.

Billy participated in Project Longhorn. In March and April, 1952, Project Longhorn, a joint Army and Air Force maneuver, took place in a vast 1,800 square mile area in Texas. Over 115,000 troops were involved. The exercise was to provide training for large-scale operations, night operations, and tactical air operations where atomic and chemical weapons might be used. One soldier, commenting on the operation, said, "We learned to turn out boots upside down and bang them together to shake out any scorpions that might have crawled in during the night when we were in our sleeping bags."

Billy was later stationed in Metz, France. In one of his letters from there, on November 10, 1952, he comments on his brother, Ernest, who had been in a serious automobile accident. He offers to help him and his family financially if they need it. He closed the letter by writing, "Ask them if they want any of this French perfume over here. I can get it cheap. Well, how is Dad getting along these days? I wish I was there to help him strip tobacco. I guess I had better close for now. I have to go on a parade tomorrow through Metz. Write soon and let me know how everything is. – Bill"

While her brother, Billy, was in service, Betty Lou Adcock agreed to a blind date. Her date was Joseph Bailey Darnell. Everyone called him JB. He grew up in Montgomery County, Tennessee. After they had dated for a while, they decided to elope. Betty put on a yellow dress, packed some clothes in a brown paper bag and walked down the drive. She was headed toward the highway when her mother caught her. When she realized what Betty was doing, she said, "You're not getting married in a yellow dress!"

Annie took her daughter to Averbuch's Ready to Wear in Nashville, and bought her a beautiful navy blue suit, a white blouse, and navy blue shoes for the wedding. On November 1, 1952, Betty's brother, Roy, drove to Springfield with Betty, their mother, Annie, and JB's brother-in-law, Duke James. JB joined them in Springfield. Betty and JB were married by Herman Ellis, the preacher at North Main Baptist Church.

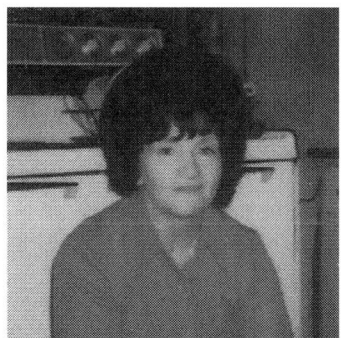

Betty and JB Darnell

After the wedding, Betty and JB went to the house they had rented. It was located off of Woodland Street, next to Vernon's Restaurant.

We, the authors of this book, are members of the generation of this family born during and after World War II. Most of us remember the precious times we spent with Gooden and Annie Adcock. We knew them as Pap and Mammy, or some variation of those names. We chose to stop our story with our parents' generation. But, we also made a promise to tell you more about the Bell Witch and about Raw Head and Bloody Bones.

When we were young, we often heard stories about the Bell Witch. Our parents and grandparents delighted in scaring the dickens out of us with such tales. The earliest appearance of the Bell Witch was in 1817. Rather than try to explain the origin, we will quote from "Goodspeed's History of Tennessee," published in 1886.

> A remarkable occurrence, which attracted wide-spread interest, was connected with the family of John Bell, who settled near what is now Adams Station about 1804. So great was the excitement that people came from hundreds of miles around to witness the manifestations of what was popularly known as the "Bell Witch." This witch was supposed to be some spiritual being having the voice and attributes of a woman. It was invisible to the eye, yet it would hold conversation and even shake hands with certain individuals. The freaks it performed were wonderful, and seemingly designed to annoy the family. It would take the sugar from the bowls, spill the milk, take the quilts from the beds, slap and pinch the children, and then laugh at the discomfiture of its victims. At first it was supposed to be a good spirit, but its subsequent acts, together with the curses with which it supplemented its remarks, proved the contrary. A volume might be written concerning the performances of this wonderful being, as they are now described by contemporaries and their descendants. That all this actually occurred will not be disputed, nor will a rational explanation be attempted. It is merely introduced as an example of superstition, strong in the minds of all but a few in those times, and not yet wholly extinct.

Mammy told the story of Pap's father, who drove his horse and buggy to Joelton one late afternoon. He was several miles down the road where he had to cross a small hill. As the buggy approached this hill, the horse reared in the air and stopped. No matter how much Pap's father encouraged the horse, it would go no further. He turned around and went home. He explained that he had encountered that crazy old Bell Witch. No one disputed him. I remember, as a young boy, my mother driving her car down this section of highway. "We're coming up on Witch Hill," she would say. Then, she accelerated a good bit beyond the posted speed limit. When we were past the hill, she slowed to normal speed. I never questioned this. I didn't dare.

These stories were passed along to us by the older generation. It is likely that these stories will not be passed along to the next generation, because the world has changed so much.

Before we tell you about Raw Head and Bloody Bones, it is important to know that, when we heard these stories, there was no social media, no television, not even a radio in the home of Gooden and Annie Adcock, because electricity did not reach them until the early 1950s. We were blessed to have experienced, for a short time, the life of the pioneer family, or very close to it. We only heard music that was live and in the moment. Our only entertainment was what we made for ourselves. One of the most exciting forms of entertainment we experienced was story-telling. And, Pap was a master story-teller.

In researching materials for this book, we asked around, and none of the cousins can remember the stories well enough to repeat them. Each of us remembers a small tidbit or a particularly gruesome detail. But, we all remember how frightened we were. John remembers Pap telling of a witch who

94

encountered a murdered man. All that was left was a pile of bloody bones and a raw bleeding head. She mumbled some words and demanded that the pile of bones rise up and dance. One by one, the bones made themselves into a skeleton and the raw head rose in the air and sat upon the bones. The head had big yellow eyes that could see in the dark. This creature waited in the shadows for naughty children who had not done their chores, or who had told a lie.

The origin of Raw Head and Bloody Bones goes back to England in the sixteenth century. We know that Pap attended only one day of school. So, he hadn't read these stories. He had heard them. They simply had to have come down to him through the generations of our family. There is no other explanation. John said, "I can tell you that, sitting on that porch with him, in the fading light, on a chilly autumn night, hearing him tell the story of Raw Head and Bloody Bones, was one of the most delightful and terrifying memories for me and my cousins."

# Chapter Twelve

# The Legacy

The Fourth Generation – Some Closure

This book begins with the earliest family members we can prove, Carter and Adelia Adcock. For the purposes of this book, we have designated them as the first generation. Their thirteen children are the second generation. We told the story of each of them, drawn from the records available to us. At that point, we narrowed our focus to Morris Riley Adcock (1840 – 1919) and his immediate family. We continued the story with his son, Morris Riley "Gooden" Adcock (1878 – 1964) and his wife, Sarah Ann "Annie" Biggs (1892 – 1978) as the third generation.

As members of the third generation, and the parents of the fourth generation in our story, Morris Riley "Gooden" Adcock and Sarah Ann "Annie" Biggs Adcock, lived a full rich life. They were married for fifty-four years. They raised a family and experienced the pleasures and pains known to all couples. They were life-long members of Bethel Church of Christ. It was said that the quality of the tobacco Gooden raised was so consistently high that he was always paid the highest price at the tobacco auction in Springfield. Gooden died at the age of eighty-six on October 31, 1964. The road leading from Whites Creek Pike to Sycamore Creek bears his name, Riley Adcock Road.

Annie Biggs Adcock and Morris Riley "Gooden" Adcock

Annie raised eleven children, ten to adulthood. She cooked on a wood stove for most of her life. She cooked three meals a day for her family. Long after most of her children were grown and married, she continued to cook about the same every day to satisfy all the grandchildren and friends who sat down to eat at her long table. She raised most of the food in her garden, kept chickens for eggs and for Sunday dinner, and always took time to listen, or to tell a good story.

From a newspaper clipping from 1975, we get a feeling for the love everyone felt for her.

> Sunday afternoon, March 9, may have been a very rainy dreary day to most folks, but for the 108 friends, neighbors and relatives of Mrs. Annie Adcock of the Forest Grove Community it was a beautiful day. At 2 p.m. they gathered at the activity building of Bethel Church of Christ to wish Mrs. Adcock a happy eighty-third birthday.
>
> Mrs. Annie, as she is known to her many friends of all ages, moved into this community when she was a little girl.
>
> Gathered around their mother for picture making were, daughters, Mrs. Betty Darnell of Forest Grove, Mrs. Jean Hansen of Florence, Alabama, Mrs. Myrtle Harris of Ashland City, Mrs. Clara Coles of Nashville, Mrs. Lorene Frazier of Pensacola, Florida, son, Roy Adcock of Madison, along with grandchildren, nieces and nephews by the score.

Annie died on February 7, 1978.

Closing the stories on the children of Gooden and Annie.

**Myrtle Louise Adcock Harris** lived in a neat white house on Bear Wallow Road, in Cheatham County. She had two daughters, Juanita and Earlene. After raising them, she raised George Howard Ruiz, the son of her oldest daughter. She had a gentle manner and a contagious sense of humor. Her warm smile could melt the coldest heart. She died on October 24, 1997.

**Clara Esther Adcock Coles** lived most of her life in Nashville. She graduated business school and raised two sons, Jesse and John. She made and collected dolls, which she enjoyed sharing with her many nieces and her granddaughter. She was bold and adventurous and always dedicated to her family. She died on August 26, 1982. Her husband, Alvin Coles, died on February 14, 1984.

**Ernest Earl Adcock** lived his life in the area around Sycamore Creek. I once heard him compared to an oak tree, as he was strong and stout. He and his wife, Annie Marshall Binkley Adcock, raised a large family. Their names are Dorothy Dean, Ernest Nelson "Bub", Lilli May, Joseph Riley "Buster", Nancy Ruth, David Earl, Mary Sue, Betty Jean, and Marsha Ann Adcock. Ernest Adcock died on November 6, 1966. Annie Marshall died on April 30, 2005.

**Ruby Frances Adcock Patterson** celebrated life with enthusiasm. Her niece, Earlene, once wrote about her, "She had such a big heart and she loved people. She was always concerned over anyone who was down on their luck or unhappy. I know we sure did get a lot of help and love from her." Ruby and her husband, George Patterson, raised three daughters, Bessie Ann, Reba, and Elaine. She enriched the lives of a generation of nephews and nieces. Ruby died on February 23, 1972. George died on May 7, 1973.

**Morris Riley Adcock** was born on March 15, 1919. He died tragically and accidentally at the age of twelve. He died on May 13, 1931.

**Hazel Lorene "Rene" Adcock Frazier** was born on May 25, 1921. She married Edward B. "Eddie" Newkirk around 1940. They were married only a short time. After enlisting in the WAVES during World War II, she married Pearlie Marvin "Boats" Frazier. They raised two daughters and a son; Utopia Ann "Topsy", Pearlie Marvin, Jr. "Skipper", and Maurene Elizabeth Frazier. Boats was a career Navy man. Rene died in Florida on July 19, 1991. Boats died in Florida on December 17, 1993. They are buried at Barrancas National Cemetery in Pensacola, Florida.

**Millard Carroll Adcock** was born on February 16, 1924. Millard never married. He worked on his parents farm his entire life. He loved to hunt and fish. He was always ready to go fishing at Sycamore Creek with any cousin, nephew or niece, or old friend who dropped by to visit. When he heard a good joke, he would usually take off his hat and slap it against his knee while laughing loudly. He was a devoted son. He died on October 27, 1985.

**Roy Wallace Adcock** was born on March 8, 1925. On November 5, 1945, he married Dorothy Virginia "Dot" Maynard. Dot was born on July 26, 1929. They had six children; Michael Stephen, Vivian Sue, Carolyn Diane, Roy Wallace, Jr., Sarah Faye, and Reba Jean Adcock. Roy worked for Robert J. Young Printing Company until he retired. Roy and Dot started D&R Letterpress after his retirement, until 2008. Roy died on December 7, 2009.

**Norma Jean Adcock Hansen** was born on June 15, 1928. She married Erick William Hansen on December 28, 1946. Jean and Erick had two daughters, Linda Clair and Carol Lynn Hansen. Erick worked in the tool and die industry in Detroit, and in Alabama. Erick died on February 6, 1999, in Florence, Alabama. After his death, Jean moved back to Tennessee, to be near her children. Jean died on August 11, 2003.

**Billy Adcock** was born on August 4, 1930. Like his brother, Millard, Bill never married and spent his life working on the family farm. He spent one enlistment in the US Army. After that, he returned to the farm. He died on June 14, 1977.

**Betty Lou Adcock Darnell** was born on October 14, 1932. She married Joseph Bailey "JB" Darnell on November 1, 1952. She had two children, an infant girl who died, and a son, Joe. They lived and worked in Springfield for a while. Betty worked for many years at the Methodist Publishing Company in Nashville. At one time, she and JB ran a small grocery store on Whites Creek Pike. It was a true "county store" where everyone in the area met and exchanged news and stories. JB died on March 23, 1986. Betty and her son, Joe, ran Honest Joe's restaurant in Joelton, until his death in 2012. Betty lives within walking distance of Sycamore Creek, next to where the old family home once stood.

In a note, Betty once wrote, "I think of the good times across the creek, wiener roasts, fishing, swimming at the old special hole. Everybody had a good time. We didn't have much, but we had love for each other. Mama seen to that."

Gooden and Annie had thirty-nine grandchildren. Born between 1932 and 1958, these grandchildren are the fifth generation living on or near Sycamore Creek. At this time, some of those grandchildren of Gooden and Annie have great grandchildren. Although we have chosen to pause our story, it is not finished. It covers seven generations who have left, and many who continue to leave, their footprints on the banks of Sycamore Creek.

# Chapter Thirteen

# The Begats

Over the years, some people have wondered why the King James' version of the Bible has all of those "begats" like those in Matthew 1. The New Standard version says "was the father of" instead of "begat." Those chapters have been described as boring by some. Matthew 1:2 says, "Abraham begat Isaac." It goes on and on from there, with the genealogy of Abraham. Of course, the purpose of the "begats" is to verify the prophecy that the Messiah would descend from Abraham. They include members of Abraham's family who explain much about Jesus, personally, socially, and politically.

Some people skip over those chapters in the Bible. You may skip this chapter, but you will miss some very interesting people. This chapter lists those people who were "begat" by Carter and Adelia Adcock. It includes their children, grandchildren, and great-grandchildren. It shows the many connections between the Adcock, Smiley, Barnes, Railey, and other families who settled in Davidson and Robertson Counties in those early times.

This chapter is not a story, but it is the framework upon which all of the stories exist. The people in this chapter define who we are as a family. They are the ones who went before and who influenced the beliefs and values of the ones who followed. Without the people listed in this chapter, we would not exist.

One very significant problem in documenting the family line is the loss of the 1890 Federal Census. It was a very detailed census that recorded information that had not been collected in earlier years. It would have provided us with answers to many questions about the family members. The 1890 Federal Census was stored on pine benches in the basement of the Commerce Building in Washington, D.C. On January 10, 1921, a devastating fire broke out. What wasn't burned, was destroyed by the water used to put out the fire.

The family expanded with each new generation. With so many family lines to follow, taking them one-at-a-time makes things easier to understand. We begin by saying, Carter and Adelia Adcock begat Nancy Adcock.

## Nancy Adcock (1819- c. 1888)

Nancy was mentioned first in her father's Last Will and Testament. Carter Adcock seemed to make an effort to name his children in their birth order, especially the older ones. There is a female under the age of ten listed in the Carter Adcock household in the 1820 Federal Census. We have no definitive documentation that shows her birth, but we believe she was born in late 1819 or early 1820.

According to Carter Adcock's Will, Nancy first married John Anderson. It is likely they married around 1835. They had a son named Carter Lee Anderson, born May 10, 1836. We have nothing that gives us any indication of what happened to John Anderson. Nancy married Luther M. Barnes in Davidson County on November 5, 1845. Luther Barnes was born about 1817, in North Carolina.

Nancy Adcock Barnes[5]                     Luther Barnes[6]

A document called "Selected U.S. Federal Census Non-Population Schedule" for 1880, describes the farm of Luther Barnes. He owned 15 acres of tilled land and 25 acres of woodland. It was valued at $400. The farm machinery he owned was valued at $25, and his live stock was valued at $150. He claimed $25 in expenses for building and repairing fences in 1879.

He had one horse, four pigs, two milk cows, and three other cows. From these milk cows, he estimated he produced 365 pounds of butter that year. Other livestock he owned included eleven sheep and nine

---

[5] Courtesy of Lois Barnes Binkley
[6] Courtesy of Lois Barnes Binkley

lambs. He said he sold three sheep and one sheep was killed by dogs. From the sheep, he produced eight bags, or twenty pounds of fleece.

He planted four acres of Indian corn which produced 100 bushels. He also produced ten bushels of Irish potatoes and fifteen bushels of sweet potatoes. He had two acres of apple trees and two acres of peach trees. He also raised one bushel of dry beans.

From documents related to the Darby vs Adcock lawsuit, we know that Nancy was living on February 21, 1887. The Sheriff of Robertson County writes that he personally handed her and her husband, Luther, a subpoena.

In 1900, Luther Barnes was living with his son, Robert N. Barnes, in Davidson County, District 25. The census for that year tells us he was eighty-tree-years-old and a widow. We believe he died later that year.

> Nancy's son, **Carter Lee Anderson**, went by several different names. He lived with his mother and step-father in 1850, and was listed as Carter L. Barnes. In 1860, he was listed as Lee Barnes, age twenty-two. In 1870, he was living near Sycamore Creek, in Robertson County, with his wife, Martha and five children. He was listed as C.W. Anderson. He was listed as Leander Anderson in 1880. In 1900, he was living in Davidson County, District 24, and listed as Carter Anderson. In 1910, he was seventy-four and using the name William Anderson. He was widowed and lived on Marrowbone Road in Davidson County, District 14. His death record gives his name as Lee Andrew Anderson. He died, at age 81, on December 1, 1915. This record lists his father as John Anderson, and his mother as Miss Adcock.

Nancy and Luther Barnes had four children, Robert N. Barnes, Sarah Dillie Barnes, Catherine "Catie" Barnes, and John Frank Barnes.

> **Robert Nathaniel Barnes** was born on September 26, 1848. He married Malinda Adcock on March 21, 1872. They had a son, Edmund S. Barnes. Malinda died around 1875. On December 14, 1876, Robert married Martha Ann Raymer. In 1900, Robert N. Barnes, was living with his second wife, Martha. Living with them was their thirteen-year-old daughter, Martha L. Barnes, and Robert's father, Luther Barnes. In 1910, Robert was living in Davidson County, District 13, on Bull Run Creek Road. With him was his wife, Martha and a hired hand. Robert N. Barnes died at this place on August 8, 1911. He was buried in the family burial ground on Bull Run Creek Road.

> **Sarah Dillie Barnes**, was born in August, 1849, in Robertson County. She married Wesley Hamilton "Ham" Knight in Cheatham County, on September 26, 1880. Their daughter, Nancy Knight, was born on July 17, 1881. Their son, Martin Wesley Knight, was born in 1883. Their son, Luther Ephram Knight, was born on June 27, 1887. Dillie's husband died in Joelton, on

November 20, 1909. Dillie was living with her sons, Wesley and Luther on Pinnacle Road, near Pleasant View, Tennessee, in Cheatham County in 1910. She died on September 15, 1905.

**Catherine "Catie" Barnes**, was born on February 18, 1854. She married Charles "Charley" Biggs in Cheatham County, on April 28, 1879. Their first son, James Monroe Biggs, was born on July 25, 1880. Their second son, Rubin Franklin Biggs, was born in Ashland City, Tennessee, on September 22, 1887. Joseph C. Biggs was born in 1891. On May 27, 1892, they had a daughter, named Alice Naomi Biggs. Leonard L. Biggs, their fourth son, was born on March 9, 1894. In 1900, they all lived in Cheatham County, District 2. Catie Barnes Biggs died sometime before 1915. Her husband, Charley Biggs married Hannah H. Walker in Cheatham County, on June 13, 1915.

**John Frank Barnes**, married Rosetta Cagle in Cheatham County on May 25, 1876. She was known as Zettie. They had fifteen children; Ella, Robert, Alice, William, Bettie, Jesse, John Frank, infant, Ida, Robert Frank, Gilbert, Johnny, Odis, Edwin, and Rosie Louella Barnes. John Frank Barnes was a blacksmith. He died on November 3, 1922. His wife, Zettie, died less than two weeks later, on November 16, 1922. They are buried at New Hope Church Cemetery.

# Anderson Adcock (1820-1896)

Anderson Adcock was born on November 10, 1820. He married Caroline Smiley on June 14, 1849. Caroline, who was born on October 29, 1831, was the daughter of Sam Smiley and Hessie Ann Warren. Anderson and Caroline Adcock had ten children.

**Artemisa Elizabeth Adcock**, who was called Missie, was born in May, 1850. She married Henry C. Tate on October 22, 1874. Henry Tate served with the 16th Regiment, Tennessee Infantry, during the Civil War. They had four children; Valeria Belle Tate, Caroline Elizabeth "Betsy" Tate, Enoch Henry Tate, and Anderson Tate. Henry died around 1904. Missie died of influenza on March 2, 1923. She was buried in the Tate Graveyard located at 1070 Walker Road, in Robertson County, Tennessee.

**Hessie Ann Adcock** was born on February 28, 1852. She married William Etheridge Tinnin in Robertson County, on September 10, 1885. Hessie and William had two children; Caroline "Callie" Tinnin, and John Tyler Tinnin. William was born on April 4, 1842. He served in Company B, Tennessee 18th Infantry Regiment. He died on April 20, 1921 in Goodlettsville, Tennessee. Hessie Ann died on March 15, 1936. They are both buried in the Tinnin Cemetery in Goodlettsville, Tennessee.

**Martha Jane Adcock** was born on November 2, 1854, at Ridgetop, in Robertson County, Tennessee. She married Samuel Washington Baxter on August 30, 1872. They had eleven children; Eugene, Thomas Jefferson, Fannie, Zella, Lallie, Samuel Washington, Jr., Sally, Zollie, Cleve, Mattie S., and Louis Filmore "Lonie" Baxter. Sam Baxter was born on November 13, 1847. He died in Joelton, Tennessee, on December 7, 1927. Martha died on December 15, 1931. They are both buried at Forest Grove Cemetery in Joelton, Tennessee.

**Sylvanus Benton "Sill" Adcock** was born in April, 1856. He married Jackie Lou Wilkerson in Davidson County, Tennessee, on January 2, 1881. Sill and Jackie had three children; Anderson Benton, Nick Franklin, and Mary Elizabeth Adcock. Jackie was born in April, 1861. She died in Greenbrier, Tennessee, on February 3, 1940. She is buried at Spring Hill Cemetery, on Dividing Ridge Road, at Ridgetop, in Robertson, County, Tennessee. Sill died before 1910. It is likely he is buried with other members of his family at Spring Hill Cemetery.

**Eveline "Eva" Adcock** was born in 1859, at Ridgetop, in Robertson County, Tennessee. She married George Greer on October 3, 1884. George was born on February 19, 1854. Edie and George had two children; Joseph Elmer, and George Moses Greer. George Greer died on April 19, 1917. He is buried at Ivy Point Church of Christ Cemetery in Goodlettsville, Tennessee.

**Mary Ellen Adcock** was born on November 18, 1861. On February 5, 1888, she married James Thomas Pyles. They had three children; Rosie L., Talitha May, and Jesse Menees Pyles. James Thomas Pyles was born about 1857. He was the son of Joseph Pyles and Louisa Reeder Pyles. He died at Greenbrier, Tennessee, on June 4, 1936. Mary Ellen died of pneumonia on May 10, 1945. They are buried at Rock Springs Cemetery, in Robertson County, Tennessee.

**Caroline "Callie" Adcock** was born on May 21, 1864. In 1900 and 1910, Callie is living with her mother, Caroline, and her brother, Taylor Adcock. She continued to live with her brother after her mother died in 1916. Callie never married. When Callie died, on July 24, 1946, Taylor was named Executor of her estate. She is buried in the Adcock Cemetery (Anderson Adcock Cemetery) at Ridgetop.

**Tyler B. Adcock** was born on January 17, 1867. She married James Thomas Greer on April 26, 1891. James was born on March 20, 1861. He was the brother of George Greer, who married Tyler's sister, Eva Adcock. Tyler and James had six children; Ida Ray, Goodlett W., Allen Floyd, Willard Marion, Pauline, and Philip Glenn Greer. James Greer died on May 19, 1933. Tyler died on May 4, 1939. They are buried at Ivy Point Church of Christ Cemetery in Goodlettsville, Tennessee.

**Talitha Adcock** was born on May 30, 1869. She was eighteen when she died on June 23,

1887. She is buried in the Adcock Cemetery (Anderson Adcock Cemetery) at Ridgetop.

**Taylor Adcock,** the youngest child of Anderson and Caroline Adcock, was born in February, 1873. He never married. He died on December 25, 1956, at Ridgetop, in Robertson County, Tennessee. At the time of his death, he was living on Dividing Ridge Road, near Goodlettsville. He is buried in the Adcock Cemetery (Anderson Adcock Cemetery).

Anderson Adcock Family photo taken around 1915.

Front row from left: Hessie Adcock Tinnin, Missie Adcock Tate, Caroline Smiley Adcock. Back row from left: Taylor Adcock, Tyler Adcock Greer, Caroline Adcock, Mary Adcock Pyles, Martha Adcock Baxter.

Caroline Smiley Adcock died of bronchial pneumonia, at the age of eighty-four, on March 31, 1916. She is buried in the Adcock Cemetery (Anderson Adcock Cemetery) at Ridgetop.

Anderson Adcock died on April 6, 1896. He is buried in the Adcock Cemetery (Anderson Adcock Cemetery).

Headstone of Caroline and Anderson Adcock

## Robert Taylor Adcock (1822-1879)

Robert Taylor Adcock was born on February 1, 1822. He married Mary Ann "Polly" Railey on December 19, 1850. Robert and Polly had eight children.

**Melinda Adcock** was born about 1855. She married Robert Nathanial Barnes on March 21, 1872. The marriage was performed by Isaac W. Rawls, Justice of the Peace in Robertson County. They had one son, Edmund Samuel Barnes. Melinda died about 1875. Their son was taken in by his paternal grandfather, Luther Barnes, and Luther's wife, Nancy Adcock Barnes. Nancy was the daughter of Carter and Adelia Adcock.

**Carter Edward Adcock** was born on January 1, 1856. He married Elizabeth "Bettie" Ann Pyles on March 20, 1881. Bettie was born about 1853, and was the daughter of Joseph and Louisa J. Reeder Pyles. Carter and Bettie had two children; John Edward, and Isaac Newton Adcock. Carter died at Greenbrier, Tennessee, on April 26, 1915. Bettie died at the home of her sister, Mary J. Kepley, in Springfield, Tennessee, on December 25, 1937. Carter and Bettie are buried at Rock Springs Cemetery in Robertson County, Tennessee.

**John Franklin Adcock** was born on March 28, 1858. He married Henrietta "Edie" Reeder on May 20, 1886. Edie was born on January 8, 1868. John and Edie had seven children; Ollie Ellis, Robert Taylor, Mike Carnie, Adis Hugh, Ben Franklin, Bonnie "Bon" Bailey, and Lillie Mae Adcock. Edie died on December 5, 1939. John died of pneumonia on May 10, 1945. They are buried at Rock Springs Cemetery in Robertson County, Tennessee.

John Adcock on left, and his children.
Left to right: Robert, Ollie, Mike, Lillie, Adis, Ben and Bon

**Cordelia "Adelia" Ann Adcock** was born on June 22, 1861. She married Cebert Stephen Smiley on October 14, 1881. Cebert was the son of Sam and Hessie Warren Smiley. He was born on February 18, 1850. They had six children; Mattie, Cebert "Buster", James, Henderson, Mary Frances, and Caroline Blanch "Callie" Smiley. Cebert died on September 23, 1915, at Greenbrier, Tennessee. Adelia died at the age of 98, on July 21, 1959. They are buried at Spring Hill Cemetery at Ridgetop, in Robertson County, Tennessee.

Family of Cebert and Adelia Smiley on the occasion of the marriage of their daughter, Mattie, to Benton Adcock on January 4, 1903

Front Row: Sammie (son of Cebert's brother Sam Smiley), Henderson, Cebert, Mary Frances, Adelia holding Callie

Second Row, Standing: Benton Adcock, Mattie Smiley Adcock, Buster, James

On Horses: Cebert's brothers, Dave Smiley and Sam Smiley

One reason it is hard to sort out the Adcock and Smiley families is illustrated by this photograph. Sam Smiley (on right horse) married Lemmie Adcock, who was the sister of Adelia Adcock Smiley. Sam and Lemmie had a son named Sammie Smiley in 1888. Lemmie died in childbirth. Cebert and Adelia Adcock Smiley took Sammie to raise. Cebert's and Adelia's daughter, Mattie Smiley, the bride in this photograph, married Benton Adcock, who was the son of Sill and Jackie Adcock. Sill's father was Anderson Adcock, the brother of Robert Adcock. And, yes, Anderson Adcock married Caroline Smiley, who was Cebert Smiley's sister. And, Cebert's other brother (on left horse) married Mary Francis Adcock, who was the sister of Robert and Anderson Adcock. Not in this photograph is Cebert's sister, Mary Francis Smiley, who married Riley Adcock, the brother of Robert and Anderson Adcock. We suggest an aspirin before you continue.

**Mary Ida Adcock** was born on May 12, 1864. She married John Alexander "Book" Raley on May 23, 1882. They moved to Boxville, in Union County, Kentucky. They had eleven children; John Freeman, Claud, Roy Hicks, Ira Gipp, Essie L., Ellis D., Mary L., Lottie, and Muriel. One of their sons lived only a short while and was not named. Mary Ida died in Boxville, Kentucky on August 14, 1914. Book died in 1925. They are buried at McClure Cemetery in Boxville, Kentucky.

John Alexander "Book" Raley and Mary Ida Adcock Raley

**Laminzer "Lemmie" Adcock** was born about 1867. She married Samuel Smiley on July 12, 1887, in Robertson County, Tennessee. Sam Smiley was born about 1847, the son of Samuel Smiley, Sr., and Hessie Ann Warren. Lemmie died in 1888 during the birth of their only son, Sammie.

**Robert Henderson "Hen" Adcock** was born in July, 1870. He married Adaline "Addie" Tennessee Smith on May 2, 1907. Addie was born in Greenbrier, Tennessee on December 27, 1886. Hen and Addie had one child, Bertha Adcock, who died in Joelton, Tennessee, in September, 1988. Hen died before 1930. On September 8, 1931, Addie married Hen's cousin, Vernon Adcock, son of Collins Adcock and Alice Knight Adcock.

**Gip Taylor Adcock** was born on July 28, 1872. He married Martha Cheat Spain on December 25, 1903. Martha Cheat Spain was born on August 4, 1881, in Greenbrier, Tennessee. They had no children of their own, but they raised a young boy named Ray D. Lassiter. He is listed as an orphan in their home in 1930. In her Last Will, Cheat stated that Ray was a good son and she loved him as though she had given birth to him. Gip died of paralysis on February 11, 1944. Cheat died in 1959. They are buried in Rock Springs Cemetery in Robertson County, Tennessee.

Martha Cheat Spain Adcock and Gip Taylor Adcock

Robert Taylor Adcock died on January 21, 1880, and is buried at the Carter Adcock Cemetery on the old Walker place. His wife, Polly Railey Adcock, died on January 9, 1905, and is buried at Rock Springs Cemetery.

# Franklin Adcock (1824-1907)

Franklin Adcock was born on October 25, 1824. He married Nancy Jane Wilson on August 30, 1866, in Cheatham County, Tennessee. Nancy was born in Georgia, in 1850. She was the daughter of Edward Wilson and Elizabeth Burlinson Wilson. We have written much about Franklin in earlier chapters. Franklin and Jane had seven children; Annie, Almeda, Elizabeth, Edward F., Carrington Jackson "Bibb", Burlinson, and Thomas Overton Adcock. Franklin's first wife, Jane Wilson Adcock, apparently left him between 1893 and 1899, and moved to Texas to live with her father. An obituary for her father, Edward Wilson, appeared in 1923, and mentioned that he was survived by several children, including Mrs. J. Adcock. We don't know when or where Jane Wilson Adcock died.

**Annie Adcock** was born about 1868. She appears in the 1870 and 1880 Federal Census. We cannot find any other documentation on her.

**Almeda Adcock** was born in April, 1870. She married Mal Walker in 1898. Mal was born in April, 1854, in Georgia. According to the 1900 Federal Census, they had one child who died. After 1900, they had three children; David S., Robert, and John W. Walker. Mal Walker died in 1911. Almeda married Calvin McClain Brooks in 1912. Almeda and Calvin had three children; Elizabeth, James, and Maudie Lee Brooks.

**Elizabeth Adcock** was born in 1873. She appears only on the 1880 Federal Census.

**Edward F. Adcock** was born about 1875. He appears only on the 1880 Federal Census.

**Carrington Jackson Adcock** was born on August 29, 1877. He married Minnie Jane Biggs, sister of Annie Biggs Adcock, on June 7, 1901. Minnie was born in August, 1889. She was the daughter of William Carrol Biggs and Julia Ann Capps. Minnie and Jack had eleven children; James Levi, Annie Mai, George M., Aaron, Jackson, Theodore, Arthur Lawrence, Julia Ethel, Effie, Clarence Carter, and Marie L. Adcock. Jack died on November 22, 1955. Minnie died on August 15, 1964. Jack and Minnie are buried at Forest Grove Cemetery in Joelton, Tennessee.

**Burlinson Adcock** was born in June, 1886. He was named for his grandmother, Elizabeth Burlinson. He appears only in the 1900 Federal Census for Cheatham County, Tennessee.

**Thomas Overton Adcock** was born on August 3, 1892. He married Jessie Elizabeth "Lizzie" Elam on May 22, 1920. They had six children; Jane, Leonard Carson, Ama Belle, Ewing Thomas, Frances, and Marie Adcock. Thomas died of apoplexy and advanced tuberculosis on August 16, 1941. His wife, Lizzie, died on January 5, 1998, at age 96. They are buried at Spring Hill Cemetery at Ridgetop in Robertson County, Tennessee.

On January 26, 1899, Franklin married Mary Jane Heriges in Cheatham County, Tennessee. Franklin and Mary Heriges had no children. Mary died in Joelton, Tennessee, on February 10, 1934. Franklin died on April 3, 1907.

Marriage record of Franklin Adcock and Mary Jane Heriges

## Cynthia Adcock (1834-1889)

Cynthia Adcock was born on March 18, 1834. She married Currington J. "C.J." Williams on July 30, 1854. We have already written much about Cynthia and C.J. because they were so involved in the William Darby vs. Franklin Adcock case.

They had three children; James, Elizabeth, and an unnamed baby who died. In 1900, C.J. was living with his daughter, Elizabeth, in Robertson County, Tennessee. He was listed as a mail carrier. C.J. died on July 10, 1900. Cynthia died on August 30, 1889. They are buried at the Carter Adcock Cemetery on the old Walker place.

> **James Williams** was born in June, 1860. He died young. He does not appear in the 1870 Federal Census.

> **Elizabeth Williams** was born on November 17, 1861. She married J.W. Miller on September 28, 1887, in Robertson County, Tennessee. Their marriage bond was signed by Elizabeth's father, C.J. Williams. Elizabeth and J.W. had two children; Dora, and Mary Miller. The 1900 Federal Census lists Elizabeth as a widow. In 1940, she was living with her daughter, Dora Miller Cole. Elizabeth died on December 16, 1954, at the age of 93. She is buried at Woodlawn Cemetery in Nashville, Tennessee.

## John C. Adcock (1836-1916)

John C. Adcock was born on January 19, 1834. John never married. He lived with his brothers, Collins and William, in the house that his father built. When his brother, Collins, married Alice Knight, John lived with them. John died of La Grippe on February 1, 1916. La Grippe was a name used for influenza at the time. He is buried at the Carter Adcock Cemetery on the old Walker place.

## Albert Adcock (1835-1869)

Albert Adcock was born about 1835. He married Rosanna "Rosy" Oaks on March 22, 1865. Albert and Rosy had two children; Madora and Ed Adcock. Albert and Rosy died about 1869. We believe they are buried at the Carter Adcock Cemetery on the old Walker place.

> **Madora Adcock** was born about 1865. We have told her story earlier. When she was about five-years-old, her parents died. She was raised by her paternal grandparents, Carter and Adelia Adcock. She married William Darby on December 13, 1885. They had one daughter, Laura Genora Darby. Madora died on December 20, 1886. We believe she is buried at the Carter Adcock Cemetery on the old Walker place.

> **Ed Adcock** was born on March 13, 1867. He married Louisa Pentecost on October 17, 1892, in Robertson County, Tennessee. They had two sons, Ed Adcock, who was born on July 6, 1895, and John Isaac Adcock, who was born on November 20, 1897. On May 4, 1916, Ed died in Nashville of Heart Disease.

## Will Adcock (1836-1897)

Will Adcock was born in 1836. He lived with his parents, then in the same house with his brothers, John and Collins, after his parents died. He married Fannie Biggs in Cheatham County on October 21, 1886. The marriage bond was signed by him and his brother Collins Adcock.

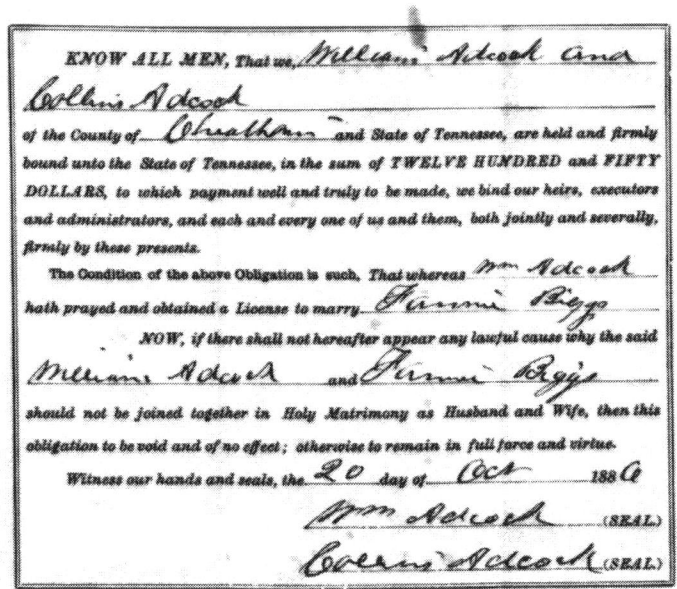

Will Adcock and Fannie Biggs Marriage Bond

He died in 1897. He is buried at Forest Grove Cemetery in Joelton, Tennessee.

Headstone of Will Adcock

## Martha Matilda Adcock (1837-1881)

Martha Matilda Adcock was born in 1837. She had a daughter, Laura Linda Adcock. Laura's father is unknown. She was raised by Martha's parents, Carter and Adelia Adcock.

> **Laura Linda Adcock** was born on March 5, 1862. Laura married Benjamin S. Darby on November 17, 1881. Benjamin was born in England. What happened to Benjamin Darby is unknown. Laura married Dr. John Bainbridge on April 27, 1886. Dr. Bainbridge was born in 1815. When he married Laura, he was a seventy-year-old widow with eight grown children. Laura and Dr. Bainbridge had two children; Naomi and Oscar Bainbridge. From 1890-1898, Dr. Bainbridge is listed in the Nashville City Directories as a physician living on Maple Street near Hyde's Ferry Pike, in Nashville. Dr. Bainbridge died on October 28, 1899. He is buried at Mount Olivet Cemetery in Nashville, Tennessee. Laura died of apoplexy on March 1, 1927, in Nashville, Tennessee. She is buried at Mount Olivet Cemetery.

Martha married John W. Hatfield on January 3, 1866. John W. Hatfield was born around 1828. On the 1870 Federal Census, he said he was born in Tennessee. On the 1880 Federal Census, he said he was born in France. We do know that Martha and John Hatfield had six children; John Henry, Mary E., Albert Carter, James H., Dillie J., and Fanny Hatfield.

**John Henry Hatfield** was born on December 11, 1866. He married Mary Lavina Settles. She was born on January 10, 1871. They had two children; Luster M., and Horace Hatfield. John Henry Hatfield died on May 28, 1926. His wife, Mary, died on October 20, 1957. They are buried in Turnersville Cemetery in Robertson County, Tennessee.

**Albert Carter Hatfield** was born on April 23, 1868. He married Mary Ann Wooten on August 19, 1897. Mary was born on April 20, 1878. They had one child, Roy C. Hatfield. Albert Carter Hatfield died of Dropsy on June 19, 1916. Mary died on February 7, 1964. They are buried at Red River Cemetery in Adams, Tennessee.

**Mary Elizabeth Hatfield** was born on February 29, 1870. She married Christopher Columbus "Lum" Shie in 1893. Lum was born July 3, 1869. They had no children. Lum died on April 4, 1943. Mary died on December 18, 1947. They are buried at Forest Grove Cemetery in Joelton, Tennessee.

**James C. Hatfield** was born on October 19, 1871. He married Nora Lee Overstreet on January 15, 1899, in Robertson County, Tennessee. James was a Town Marshal in Adams, Tennessee, at the time of his death. James died on July 31, 1936 in Adams, in Robertson County, Tennessee. James and Nora had three children; Durard, Vera, and James Hatfield.

**Dillie J. Hatfield** was born on April 10, 1874. She married William David Hunter in Robertson County, Tennessee, on April 27, 1899. William was born on July 27, 1877. They had five children; James, Wallace, Jessie, Orville, and Oscar. Dillie died on January 2, 1929. She is buried at Elmwood Cemetery in Springfield, Tennessee. William Hunter died on April 20, 1959. He is buried at Springfield Memorial Gardens in Springfield, Tennessee.

**Fanny Hatfield** was born about 1870. She was named in the William Darby vs. Franklin Adcock case, so she was about seventeen-years-old at that time. She does not appear in the 1900 Federal Census.

# Elizabeth Adcock (1838-1919)

Elizabeth "Bettie" Adcock was born on December 22, 1838. She married James Thomas Cooper on September 7, 1862. James was born in New York, on December 25, 1836. His family moved to Fentress, Tennessee. When they moved to Nashville, they brought young Rosy Oakes with them. Rosy married Albert Adcock, Bettie Adcock's brother. Bettie and James had five children; William E., Mary Margaret, James Thomas, Jr., Elizabeth, and Emma Cooper. James died on April 2, 1876. He is buried at Mount Olivet Cemetery, in Nashville, Tennessee. Bettie was a widow with five children.

**William E. Cooper** was born about 1863. In the 1880 Federal Census, he is at home, working on the farm with his mother. The other children are listed as "in school." He does not appear after the 1880 Federal Census.

**Mary Margaret Cooper** was born in 1865. She does not appear after the 1880 Federal Census.

**James Thomas Cooper, Jr.** was born on May 1, 1867, in Joelton, Tennessee. He married Rosa Henderson in 1892. James and Rosa had seven children; James Arthur, Hauley Edward, Myrtle, Emma, Howard, Buford Ray, and Evelyn Cooper. James died on January 15, 1942. Rosa died on August 11, 1967. They are buried at Forest Grove Cemetery in Joelton, Tennessee.

**Elizabeth Cooper** was born in 1869. She does not appear after the 1880 Federal Census.

**Emma Cooper** was born in 1874. Emma married Horace D. Elliott in 1898. Horace was born in Greenwood, Minnesota on January 22, 1876. In 1900, Horace and Emma lived near Bettie and Laura in Davidson County, District 24. Between 1902 and 1905, Emma and Horace moved to Rockford Minnesota. By 1909, they had moved to Oregon. Emma and Horace had four children; Robert George, Alfred R., Edison H., and Vernon C. Elliott. In 1918, Horace registered for the WWI draft in Los Angeles, California. Horace died in Los Angeles, California, on July 3, 1919. Emma was living in Los Angeles, with her son, Robert G. Elliott in 1920. She does not appear on the 1930 Federal Census.

On November 2, 1887, Elizabeth Adcock Cooper adopted Laura Genora Darby, the daughter of Madora and William Darby. She committed to make Laura equal to her other children and to raise her with every benefit afforded her own children.

**Laura Genora Darby Cooper** was born on October 12, 1886. She married William Grandville Towns on December 22, 1905. William was born on October, 16, 1878. They had nine children; Roscoe Grandville, Dorothy Mai, Anna, Ruby Florence, Willie Bea, Brownie Kingsley, Norman Ivan, Hazel Marie, Lucille, Lawrence Robert, and Geraldine. William died on August 14, 1938. Laura died on September 21, 1973. They are buried at Webb Cemetery in Joelton, Tennessee.

William G. Towns        Laura Genora Towns

Elizabeth Adcock Cooper died on March 16, 1919. She is buried at Forest Grove Cemetery in Joelton, Tennessee.

## Morris Riley Adcock (1840-1919)

Morris Riley Adcock was born on October 22, 1840. He married Mary Frances Smiley on April 11, 1867. Mary Frances Smiley was born on January 15, 1840. She was the daughter of Samuel Smiley and Hessie Ann Warren Smiley.

Marriage License of Morris Riley Adcock and Mary Frances Smiley

Riley and Mary had four children; David, Collins B., William A. "Will", and Morris Riley "Gooden" Adcock, Jr. Mary Frances died on September 19, 1909. Riley Adcock died on March 24, 1919. They are buried at Forest Grove Cemetery in Joelton, Tennessee.

Morris Riley Adcock

**David "Dave" Adcock** was born on February 15, 1869. David never married. David died of Typhoid Fever at Dr. Dozer's Infirmary on August 15, 1924. He is buried at Forest Grove Cemetery in Joelton, Tennessee.

**Collins B. Adcock** was born on February 4, 1871. He never married. He died on September 14, 1893. He is buried at Forest Grove Cemetery in Joelton, Tennessee.

**William A. "Will" Adcock** was born on August 16, 1873. Will married Laura Chambliss about 1901. Laura was born on December 8, 1885. They had eight children; William M., Elsie, Mary Frances, Pauline, Milton B., an infant that was still born in 1917, Margaret Elizabeth, and Agathea Adcock. Will died of a bullet wound on June 17, 1937. Laura died of a heart attack at Vanderbilt University Hospital in Nashville, Tennessee, on June 8, 1958. They are buried at Forest Grove Cemetery in Joelton, Tennessee.

**Morris Riley "Gooden" Adcock, Jr.** was born on May 28, 1878. He married Sarah Ann "Annie" Biggs on April 10, 1910. Annie was born on March 9, 1892, the daughter of William Carroll Biggs and Julia Ann Capps Biggs. Gooden and Annie had eleven children; Myrtle Louise, Clara Esther, Ernest Earl, Ruby Frances, Morris Riley, Hazel Lorene "Rene", Millard Carroll, Roy Wallace, Norma Jean, Billy, and Betty Lou Adcock. Gooden died on October 31, 1964. Annie died on February 7, 1978. They are buried at Forest Grove Cemetery.

## Mary Frances Adcock (1848-1913)

Mary Frances Adcock was born on March 14, 1848. She married David Smiley on around 1864. David Smiley was born on February 11, 1837, the son of Samuel Smiley and Hessie Ann Warren Smiley. Mary and Dave had eight children; Lewis, Elijah, James, Carter, Samuel, Albert "Kit", David C., and Joseph Smiley. Mary died on June 2, 1913. Dave died on November 26, 1915. They are buried at Spring Hill Cemetery at Ridgetop, in Robertson County, Tennessee.

**Lewis Smiley** was born in 1867. He appears in the 1870 and 1880 Federal Census.

**Elijah Smiley** was born in February, 1870. He only appears on the 1870 Federal Census.

**James Smiley** was born on September 8, 1871. He married Mary Mollie Tate on October 24, 1894. Mary was born on August 13, 1877, the daughter of Frank T. Tate and Sarah "Sally" Smiley Tate. James and Mary had seven children; Sallie, Charlie, Dave Dorylin, Allie, Hessie Fiarie, Ora L., and Carrie Belle Smiley. James and Mary are buried at Spring Hill Cemetery in Ridgetop, in Robertson County, Tennessee.

**Carter Smiley** was born was born in 1873. He married Johnnie Ella Mathews on April 23, 1905. Ella was born in March, 1882, in Georgia. Carter and Ella had five children; Rudie B., Clyde D., Nellie A., Nannie, and John Carter Smiley. Carter died in 1946. His headstone says he was born in 1868, but he does not appear on the 1870 Federal Census. Ella died in 1970. They are buried at Spring Hill Cemetery at Ridgetop, in Robertson County, Tennessee.

**Albert "Kit" Smiley** was born on June 22, 1876. He married Mozzella Evie Paradise, the daughter of Ike Paradise. Her mother's name was Tate. Albert and Mozzella had two children; William and Maggie Smiley. Albert died on February 11, 1945. Mozzella died on September 5, 1949. They are buried at Spring Hill Cemetery at Ridgetop, in Robertson County, Tennessee.

**David C. Smiley** was born on May 7, 1877. He married Mary E. Adcock about 1903. Mary E. Adcock was born on August 23, 1887, the daughter of Sylvanus Adcock and Jackie Wilkerson. David and Mary had three children; Jackie L., Elmer Clarence, and Rosie C. Smiley. David died on June 30, 1924. He is buried at Spring Hill Cemetery at Ridgetop, in Robertson County, Tennessee. Mary married Enoch Henry Tate on February 25, 1930. Enoch was the son of Henry C. Tate and Artemisa "Missie" Adcock. Enoch died on October 15, 1944. He is buried at Spring Hill Cemetery at Ridgetop, in Robertson County, Tennessee. Mary died on September 5, 1971. She is buried next to her first husband, David C. Smiley, at Spring Hill Cemetery at Ridgetop, in Robertson County, Tennessee.

**Joseph Smiley** was born on October 11, 1878. Joseph never married. On his draft card for WWI, he states he is missing one finger. He died in 1969, and is buried at Spring Hill Cemetery at Ridgetop, in Robertson County, Tennessee.

## Collins Adcock (1850-1929)

Collins Adcock was born on April 22, 1850. Mary Rebecca Adcock Binkley, daughter of Collins and Alice Knight Adcock, said that her father hid photographs in the walls of their house. The photographs were of her father, Collins, and a woman named Julia Chambliss. Julia, known as "Lulu", was born in Robertson County, on August 12, 1852. Mary said that Collins and Julia had three sons; Henry, born in 1871, John Lacel, born in 1876, and William, born in May, 1880. Julia Chambliss married Edward Raymer on December 2, 1880. The three boys kept their mother's maiden name, Chambliss. Henry married Mary Ellen Adcock on March 17, 1891. She was the daughter of Clay Adcock and Sally Knight. John Lacel Chambliss was born on February 8, 1876. He married Thresa Amelia Leibfritz in 1909. Thresa was the daughter of Stephen and Benedicta Eggstein Leibfritz. William was born in 1880. We have no other information on him.

Collins married Alice Knight on April 13, 1900. Alice Knight was born on November 9, 1870. She was the daughter of Andrew Jackson Knight and Mary Rebecca Wilson Knight. When Alice married Collins, she had a son named Boss Eans. Collins and Mary had four children; Vernon, Christopher Columbus "Lum", Mary Rebecca, and Obie A. Adcock. Collins died on July 3, 1929. He is buried at the Carter Adcock Cemetery. Alice died on November 20, 1945. She is buried at Forest Grove Cemetery in Joelton, Tennessee.

Collins Adcock

**Vernon Adcock** was born on February 2, 1901. He married Adaline "Addie" Smith on September 8, 1931. Addie was born on December 27, 1886, in Greenbrier, Tennessee. She was the widow of Henderson Adcock. Bertha Adcock, the daughter of Henderson and Addie Smith Adcock, became the step-daughter of Vernon Adcock. Addie Smith Adcock died on March 5, 1965. She is buried at Mount Sharon Cemetery in Greenbrier, Tennessee. Vernon Adcock died on January 16, 1963. Vernon is buried at Forest Grove Cemetery.

**Christopher Columbus "Lum" Adcock** was born on October 7, 1903. He married Naomi Trenary in 1924. Naomi was born on April 25, 1906. Lum and Naomi had eight children; Johnnie Mae, Robert, Ida Louise, Leon Isaiah, Dorothy, Marie, Betty, and Floyd Adcock. Lum died on May 15, 1982. Naomi died on August 8, 1991. They are buried at Forest Grove Cemetery in Joelton, Tennessee.

**Mary Rebecca Adcock** was born was born on December 17, 1909, in Joelton, Tennessee. She married Carl Woodruff Binkley. Carl was born on September 1, 1916, in Cheatham County, Tennessee. Mary and Carl had two children, Bethel L., and Emery D. Binkley. Carl died on November 7, 1991. He is buried at Oakwood United Methodist Church Cemetery in

Cheatham County, Tennessee. Mary died on February 17, 2006. She is buried at Forest Grove Cemetery in Joelton, Tennessee.

**Obie A. Adcock** was born on October 5, 1910. He married Lula Burton Jones after 1940. Lula was born on November 29, 1906. Obie and Lula had no children. Lula died on November 24, 1958. Obie died on March 24, 1980. They are buried at Forest Grove Cemetery in Joelton, Tennessee.

Mary, Lum, Vernon, Collins, Alice, and Obie Adcock

# Chapter Fourteen

# Cemeteries in this Book

We have indicated the cemeteries where many of our Adcock ancestors are buried. Earlier in this book, we gave the origin of Forest Grove Cemetery, where so many of our relatives are at rest. In this chapter, we will discuss some of the other cemeteries of particular interest to the family. In one case, an old family cemetery has disappeared. Some of us living today, remember it as Graveyard Hill. We are reasonably sure that the people buried there are the children of Franklin and Jane Adcock. All traces of it have vanished, due to erosion, decay, and vandalism. In some cases, we are reasonably sure of the burial location of some ancestors, but can't state it with certainty because wooden markers rotted away years ago, or the graves were simply marked with large rocks. Some graves were never marked in any way. Written records were not always made or kept. Even when death certificates are available the location of the burial is sometimes recorded as "family burying ground" which isn't helpful when a family has more than one family cemetery.

Some of these cemeteries are very old and the stories of their origins are lost. Some have stories of their own that deserve recording. In this chapter, we look at what we know, and what we do not know about the most significant cemeteries mentioned in this book.

It is important to know which cemetery we are discussing. There has been some confusion on this subject. The Adcock Cemetery on Walker Road is where Anderson and Caroline Adcock are buried. The Adcock Cemetery, where Carter and Adelia Adcock are buried is off of Greenbrier Road, and has long been referred to as the "Adcock Cemetery on the old Walker place." The Krantz Cemetery, on Ivey Point Road, has been called the Adcock Cemetery, or the Krantz-Adcock Cemetery. So, we will make it clear which cemetery we are discussing.

In this chapter, when we refer to the Adcock Cemetery on Walker Road, we will add, in parenthesis, (Anderson Adcock Cemetery). The Adcock Cemetery off of Greenbrier Road will be called the Carter Adcock Cemetery. The Krantz-Adcock Cemetery on Ivey Point Road will be called the Krantz Cemetery.

It is important to know where these family burial grounds are located. When we give a description of their location, we consistently use one reference point and explain how to get to each cemetery from that point. In each case, that reference point is the intersection of Whites Creek Pike (U.S 431) and Interstate 24.

# Adcock Cemetery (Anderson Adcock Cemetery)

**Location:** From the intersection of Whites Creek Pike and I-24, go north on Whites Creek Pike about 1.6 miles to Greenbrier Road. Turn right. Stay on Greenbrier Road about 2.7 miles to Huffman Road. Turn right on Huffman Road. Huffman Road changes its name to Dividing Ridge Road. Stay on Dividing Ridge Road about 2 miles until you reach Walker Road. Make a sharp right turn onto Walker Road. Adcock Cemetery (Anderson Adcock Cemetery) is about .8 mile on the right. The cemetery is enclosed by a picket fence on the right side of the road. The address is approximately 1212 Walker Road.

This cemetery has a rich history. Although that history was never recorded, we can piece it together from a variety of old records. This patch of hallowed ground can be traced back to John A. Adcock and his daughter, Winney Adcock. We received communications from Yolanda Reid at the Robertson County Archives. She wrote:

> "We have a list of 12 engraved tombstones in this cemetery. Of course there is the possibility that others are buried there with no engraved stone. This is not a church cemetery, it is a family cemetery thus was owned by the family. I have tracked the land records for this property from Jack D. Walker, who purchased the farm in 1974, backwards to Anderson Adcock, who purchased it in 1847. Unfortunately, none of these deeds designated the cemetery on this property as existing until 1974, when Mr. Stenglein purchased about 30 acres from Mr. Walker. The surveys, which took place when Jack Walker began selling off small tracts, allowed us to determine the size of the cemetery. Due to the research in tracing this land, the Tax Assessor records show the cemetery as a separate parcel named Adcock Cemetery."

**Some of the Graves in Adcock Cemetery (Anderson Adcock Cemetery)**

**Anderson Adcock** (1820-1896) Anderson was the son of Carter and Adelia Adcock. He is buried next to **Caroline Smiley Adcock** (1831-1916). Caroline was the daughter of Sam and Hessie Warren Smiley. Anderson and Caroline were married in Robertson County on June 14, 1849. Caroline died on March 31, 1916, of pneumonia. She was eighty-four.

**Caroline "Callie" Adcock** (1864-1946) Callie was the daughter of Anderson and Caroline Smiley Adcock. She never married. After her mother died, she lived with her brother, Taylor Adcock. She left everything to him in her Last Will and Testament. Callie died on July 24, 1946. Her death certificate states she died of high blood pressure due to old age. She was eighty-two.

**Talitha Adcock** (1869-1887) Talitha was the daughter of Anderson and Caroline Smiley Adcock. She was only eighteen when she died, on June 23, 1887.

**Taylor Adcock** (1873-1956) Taylor was the son of Anderson and Caroline Smiley Adcock. He was single. He took care of his mother and his sister, Callie, until they died. He died in the Davidson County Hospital on Christmas Day, 1956. He was eighty-four.

**William Smiley** (1886-1910) William "Buck" Smiley was the youngest son of Joe and Eliza Harris Smiley. He died single at the age of twenty-four.

**Eliza Harris Smiley** (1843-1918) Eliza was the wife of Joe Smiley and the daughter of James and Bettie McNeal Harris. She died on June 16, 1918. She was seventy-five.

**Ewin Hampton** (1896-1911) Ewin was the son of William and Mary Smiley Hampton. His mother, Mary Fanny Smiley Hampton (1870-1942) was the daughter of Joe and Eliza Harris Smiley.

**Ike Asa Adcock** (1850-1927) Ike Adcock was the son of John Adcock and Martha Jane Arrington. He is buried by his wife, Anne Perigen. His death certificate states he was born on May 16, 1856 and died of acute heart trouble on August 26, 1928. His mother, Jane, is buried in the Krantz Cemetery on Ivey Point Road.

**Anne Perigen Adcock** (1868-1910) Anne was the wife of Ike Asa Adcock. She was the daughter of J. Lafayette and Pollie Railey Perigen.

**Lisa Palina Perigen Wingo** (1866-1897) Liza was the daughter of J. Lafayette and Pollie Railey Perigen. She married Charles Wesley Wingo, who is also buried here.

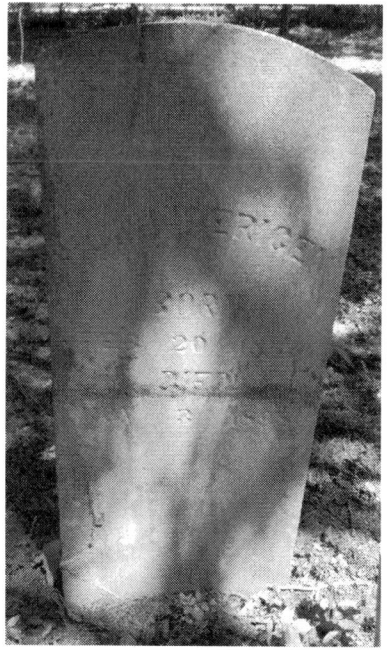

**Noah Perigen** (1875-1898) Noah Perigen was the son of J. Lafayette and Pollie Railey Perigen. He was shot in the face and killed by Frank T. Tate on November 3, 1898. Noah was twenty-three years old. On February 4, 1899, Frank Tate was indicted for first degree murder. Summoned to testify were Davis Wiley Wingo, C.W. Wingo, Ann Perigen, Liza Wingo and Joe Perigen. During the trial Isaac A. Adcock and James Rogers Adcock were deposed. On February 17, 1900, Tate was found guilty of second degree murder and sentenced to eighteen years hard labor in the State penitentiary.

Source: Robertson County Circuit Court Minutes, 1899.

 **Frank Adcock** (1887-1942) Frank was the son of Ike and Anne Perigen Adcock.

 **Ruby Johnson Adcock** (1898-1927) Ruby was the wife of Frank Adcock.

**Jesse Gilbert Adcock** (1885-1923) Jesse was the son of Ike and Anne Perigen Adcock.

**Edward Adcock** (1867-1916) Edward was the son of Albert and Rosy Oakes Adcock.

While this small cemetery contains the earthly remains of Anderson Adcock and some of his relatives, as well as Ike Adcock and some of his relatives, it does not prove a relationship between Ike Adcock and Anderson Adcock. However, it is very strong evidence of a common family link to John Adcock.

There are other family members buried in the Adcock Cemetery (Anderson Adcock Cemetery). There are certainly unmarked graves there as well.

Carolyn Adcock Smith by the headstone of Anderson and Caroline Adcock

# Carter Adcock Cemetery

**Location:** From the intersection of Whites Creek Pike and I-24, go north on Whites Creek Pike about 2.5 miles to Jackman Road. Turn right. Stay on Jackman Road about 1.5 miles until you reach Greenbrier Road. Turn left on Greenbrier Road. Go about .4 mile until you cross the bridge over the South Fork of Sycamore Creek. Just past the bridge, there is a pond on the right and, on the left, is a gravel road. Turn left onto this gravel road. This is private property, so you will need the permission of the land owner to visit this cemetery. Go back this road about .4 mile. You will have to ford Sycamore Creek. Heavy rains can make fording at this location impossible. At the end of this gravel road is a church. The Carter Adcock Cemetery is in a fenced area behind the church.

The Carter Adcock Cemetery is often referred to as the "Adcock cemetery on the old Walker place." The current owners take good care of it. Carolyn Adcock Smith visited the cemetery in 2013 to photograph some of the graves. She noted that only about six graves were marked. Others had simple rocks at the head and foot of the graves. There appeared to be sixteen to twenty grave sites.

Carolyn Adcock Smith between the graves of Carter Adcock and Adelia Railey Adcock

From a survey done on December 25, 2000, by Landon Darnell, son of the owner of the property at that time, we have the following known marked graves:

**Carter Adcock** (1801-1877) His headstone has the inscription, "Carter Adcock, born Jan 1 1801, died Nov 16 1877." Next to Carter's headstone is a grave with a large round-top stone with no markings. This is certainly the grave of his wife Adelia Railey Adcock.

**John Adcock** (1836-1916) His marker has the dates January 27, 1836-February 1, 1916. John was the son of Carter and Adelia Adcock.

**Robert Adcock** (1822-1880) His marker has his name and the dates February 1, 1822-January 21, 1880. Robert was the son of Carter and Adelia Adcock.

**Cynthia Williams** (1834-1889) Her marker has her name and the inscription, "d. Aug. 30, 1889, age 55 y, 5 mo., 12 days." Cynthia Adcock Williams was the daughter of Carter and Adelia Adcock. Her gravestone is to the right of her husband, C. J. Williams.

**CJ Williams** (1831-1900) He was the husband of Cynthia Adcock. In addition to his name, his marker is inscribed, "d. July 10, 1900, age 69 y, 6 mo. 23 days, Lieut. Co. C 40 U.S.C.I."

**Collins Adcock** (1850-1929) Collins was the son of Carter and Adelia Adcock. He married Alice Knight. His headstone is also broken with only the bottom portion remaining. One can read the birthday (April) 22, 1850. Collins' death certificate says he was buried at the Family Cemetery.

We believe that the Carter Adcock Cemetery is the location of the graves of Albert and Rosy Oaks Adcock, Madora Adcock Darby, and William Darby. Unfortunately, we can find no paper trail or grave markers to verify this belief.

Several graves have stones without inscriptions. Other graves have no marker at all. Carolyn Adcock Smith, and her granddaughter, Olivia, a seventh generation descendant of Carter and Adelia Adcock inspect the graves with inscriptions.

Carter owned land in Robertson County. On January 31, 1845, he purchased 174 acres of land in Davidson County. That land is where the Carter Adcock Cemetery is located.

# Krantz Cemetery

Location: From the intersection of Whites Creek Pike and I-24, go north on Whites Creek Pike about .8 mile to Morgan Road. Turn right. Stay on Morgan Road for 2.1 miles when Morgan Road becomes Union Hill Road. Continue straight on Union Hill Road 1 mile to Ivey Point Road. Turn left on Ivey Point Road. Go 1.1 miles to Browns Lake Road. The Krantz Cemetery is on the left on Ivey Point Road just beyond where Ivey Point Road forks with Browns Lake Road. It is approximately 3001 Ivey Point Road.

The Krantz Cemetery is part of a thirty-nine acre tract of land that once belonged to Asa Adcock. It is listed in the 10th Civil District being shown as Asa Adcock property on the tax books, Map 10, Parcel 101315. It was surveyed on August 2, 1967, by Alvin W. Thomas, Jr., as excerpted here:

> Tract No. 1 being a graveyard of the Adcock family and beginning at an iron pin on the westerly margin of Ivey Point Road and a private driveway; thence following a margin of said Ivey Point Road. According to Davidson County Deed Book 4644, pages 758-761, the land was transferred from Herman A. Krantz (1924-2006) to Anita R. Krantz (born December 9, 1921). Three tracts were transferred. One tract was the cemetery.

Some of the graves of particular interest to our story are listed below:

**Martha Jane Arrington Adcock** (1812-1904), wife of John A. Adcock (1807-1870). This is a mystery for several reasons. The earliest record for her is her marriage to John Adcock on October 30, 1834. This is in Davidson County. They were married by Dan Buie, JP. They do not appear in the 1840 census.

In the 1850 Federal Census for Davidson County, District 22, she is listed with John Adcock and their children; Varilla (18), Virginia (16), Stokely (14), Louisa (8), John E. (7), Tennessee (4), and No Name (2). We know from the next census that "No Name" was Micaga "Cage" Adcock, born in 1850. The 1860 Federal Census shows the addition of children; Hitta (8), and Isaac (5). In 1880, Jane is living with her son, John E. Adcock. With them are; Stokely (39), Cage (27) and Zack (24). Zack is listed as a "cousin." Also listed is Jim Rogers (21), a "nephew." They are living near Asa Adcock and his wife Virginia.

The 1900 census lists Jane living with her son, Stokely (60), Cage (45), and Mattie (18) a "niece." Jane died on April 24, 1904, and was buried in the Krantz Cemetery on Ivey Point Road. Her grave stone says she was 100 years old. It is not likely. Most of the records indicate she was born in 1812, which would have made her a respectable ninety-two years old.

**Bettie Ann Adcock** (1872-1931), daughter of Asa and Virginia Adcock. Died of a fractured skull received in an auto accident. Single

**Ike W Adcock** (1876-1932), son of Asa and Virginia Adcock.

Single.

**Nora Adcock Cook** (1881-1967), daughter of Asa and Virginia Adcock. She married Arthur Dorris Boone. He died in 1930. Then, she married James W. Cook.

**Matt Trenary** (1882-1914), daughter of Asa and Virginia Adcock, married George Trenary.

**Arthur Dorris Boone** (1885-1930), husband of Nora Adcock. Nora Adcock was the daughter of Asa and Virginia Adcock.

**Lena Krantz** (1891-1943), daughter of Alfred Utley and Sarah Adcock, wife of **Hubert Krantz** (1895-1990). Sarah Adcock was the daughter of Asa and Virginia Adcock.

# Spring Hill Cemetery

Location: From the intersection of Whites Creek Pike and I-24, go north on Whites Creek Pike about 1.6 miles. Turn right onto Greenbrier Road. Go forward on Greenbrier Road for 2.7 miles and turn right onto Huffman Road. A short distance on Huffman Road the name changes to Dividing Ridge Road. Continue on Dividing Ridge Road for about 2.8 miles and Spring Hill Cemetery will be on your right. Spring Hill Cemetery is about 6053 Dividing Ridge Road and just a short distance from Spring Hill Baptist Church.

Some of the graves of particular interest to our story are listed below:

**Dave Smiley** (1837-1915) husband of Mary Frances Adcock Smiley. He was the son of Sam and Hessie Warren Smiley. His wife, Mary Frances Adcock, was the daughter of Carter and Adelia Adcock.

**Mary Francis Adcock Smiley** (1840-1913) wife of David Smiley and daughter of Carter and Adelia Adcock.

**Albert "Kit" Smiley** (1876-1945) was the son of David and Mary Frances Adcock Smiley. Kit married Mozella Evie Paradise.

**Carter Smiley** (1873-1946) and his wife **Ella Matthews Smiley** (1882-1970). Carter was the son of David and Mary Frances Adcock Smiley.

**Joseph Smiley** (1878-1969) was the son of David and Mary Frances Adcock Smiley. His draft registration for World War I says he is tall, has blue eyes and light brown hair, and has one missing finger.

**Joseph Houston Smiley** (1911-1940) He was the son of Samuel Smiley and Martha Robertson Smiley.

**Thomas O. Adcock** (1892-1941) was the son of Franklin Adcock (1824-1907) and Jane Wilson Adcock (1850-unknown). He was a grandson of Carter and Adelia Adcock. He married Lizzie Elam.

**Charles S. Adams** (1898-1925), and his wife, **Hessie Ida Smiley Adams** (1906-?). Hessie's parents were James Smiley (1871-1938) and Mary Mollie Tate (1877-1933).

**James Smiley** was the son of David Smiley (1837-1915) and Mary Frances Adcock Smiley (1848-1913). He was a grandson of Carter and Adelia Adcock.

 **David D. Smiley** (1900-1971) and his wife, **Hazel Elliott Smiley** (1902-1961). David was the son of James Smiley and Mary Mollie Tate.

 **Martha Evelyn Smiley** (1884-1965) Martha Evelyn Robertson Smiley was the wife of Samuel Smiley (1888 – 1957).

 **Cebirt Smiley** (1850-1915) and **Adelia Adcock Smiley** (1861-1959). Cebirt Smiley was the son of Sam Smiley (1807-1888) and Hessie Warren Smiley (1811-1894). Adelia Adcock Smiley was the daughter of Robert Taylor Adcock (1822-1879) and Mary "Polly" Railey (1831-1905). Cebirt Smiley was a grandson of Carter and Adelia Adcock.

**James Smiley** (1854-1930) Jim Smiley was the son of Sam and Hessie Warren Smiley. He married Mary L. Brown Reavis (1872-1968). He died on September 4, 1930.

**James S. Tate** (1867-1950) Jim Tate was the son of Frank T. Tate and Sally Smiley Tate. His wife, Malinda Jane Brickley Tate (1877 – 1968) is also buried at Spring Hill Cemetery.

**Frank T. Tate** (1837-1918) Frank T. Tate was the son of Frank T. Tate, Sr. and Elizabeth Adcock Tate. He married Sally Smiley, the daughter of Sam and Hessie Warren Smiley. During the War Between the States, he served in the Confederate Infantry. He shot and killed Noah Perigen in 1898 and was convicted of second degree murder. In 1900, he was sentenced to eighteen years in prison. In 1920, he was living alone in Robertson County, District Twelve. He died of "apoplexy" on February 1, 1921. His death certificate states he was buried at his home. The memorial in Spring Hill Cemetery is not a grave marker. He is buried off of Walker Road, Ridgetop, Tennessee.

**Johnnie E. Adcock** (1915-1960) Johnnie Everett Adcock was the son of Anderson Benton Adcock (1882-1941) and Mattie Smiley Adcock (1883-1957). His wife was Lorene Callis Adcock (1920-1999).

**Pauline Adcock Morris** (1925-2005) Pauline was the daughter of Anderson Benton Adcock and Mattie Smiley Adcock. She was the wife of Joseph Morris (1921-1994).

**Earline Adcock Howard** (1925-2009) was the daugter of Anderson Benton Adcock and Mattie Smiley Adcock. She was the wife of James B. Howard (1921-1994).

**Nick Franklin Adcock** (1885-1963). Nick Franklin Adcock was the son of Sylvanus "Sill" Adcock and Jackie Wilkerson Adcock. He was the grandson of Anderson and Caroline Adcock. He married Bedie L. Hunt (1888-1947). His WWI and WWII draft records state he was born on June 12, 1884.

**James T. Tate** (1899-1992) He was the son of James S. Tate and Millie Vaughn Tate. He was the husband of **Jennie Mai Gober** (1906-1997).

# Tate Graveyard

**Directions:** From the intersection of Whites Creek Pike and I-24, go north on Whites Creek Pike about 1.6 miles to Greenbrier Road. Turn right. Stay on Greenbrier Road about 2.7 miles to Huffman Road. Turn right on Huffman Road. Huffman Road changes its name to Dividing Ridge Road. Stay on Dividing Ridge Road about 2 miles until you reach Walker Road. Make a sharp right turn onto Walker Road. Tate Graveyard is about 1.2 miles on the right. The address is approximately 1070 Walker Road. This is on the same road with the Adcock Cemetery (Anderson Adcock Cemetery) but farther down the road.

**Artemisa Adcock Tate** (1850-1923) She was the daughter of Anderson and Caroline Smiley Adcock. She married Henry C. Tate on October 22, 1874. Her death certificate states, "I thought she had influenza and I guess she died with appoplexy." It was signed by Turner L. Johnson. She died on March 2, 1923. She was seventy-two.

**Charles Dickson Trenary** (1844-1920) He was the son of William and Hezekiah Kernal Trenary. He married Elizabeth Tate, daughter of Henry and Artemisa Adcock Tate.

**Frank T. Tate** (1837-1918) Frank T. Tate married Sarah "Sally" Smiley. He was the son of Frank T. Tate, Sr. and Elizabeth Adcock McGraw Tate. He was the brother of Henry C. Tate.

**Eliza Ann Tate Sevier-Paradise** (1831-1900) She was the daughter of Frank T. Tate, Sr. and Elizabeth Adcock McGraw Tate.

**Elias "Lash" McGraw** (1829-1905) He was the son of Elijah McGraw and Elizabeth Adcock McGraw.

**Elizabeth Adcock McGraw Tate** (1807-1873) She married Elijah McGraw. They had one son, Elias "Lash" McGraw. After Elijah McGraw died, Elizabeth married Frank T. Tate, Sr.

# Rock Springs Cemetery

**Directions:** From the intersection of Whites Creek Pike and I-24, go north on Whites Creek Pike about 1.6 miles to Greenbrier Road. Go 2.9 miles. Note: Greenbrier Road becomes Edgar Dillard Road after it crosses Huffman Road. Turn left onto Betts Road (TN 257 West.) After 0.3 mile, turn left onto Rock Springs Road. Rock Springs Baptist Church is 0.6 mile. Rock Springs Cemetery is located behind the church.

**Gip Taylor Adcock** (1872-1944) He was the son of Robert Taylor and Polly Railey Adcock.

**Cheatham "Cheat" Adcock** (1881-1959) She was the daughter of Alex F. and Martha Elam Spain and the wife of Gip Taylor Adcock.

**Elizabeth Ann Pyles Adcock** (1854-1937) She was the daughter of Joseph and Louisa J. Reeder Pyles. She married Carter Edward Adcock, the son of Robert Taylor and Polly Railey Adcock.

**Carter E. Adcock** (1856-1915) He was the son of Robert Taylor and Polly Railey Adcock. He married Elizabeth "Bettie" Ann Pyles.

**John Franklin Adcock** (1858-1945) He was the son of Robert Taylor and Polly Railey Adcock.

**Henrietta Reeder Adcock** (1868-1939) She was the daughter of Benjamin and Jane Dorris Reeder and the wife of John Franklin Adcock.

**Ollie Ellis Adcock** (1892-1949) He was the son of John Franklin and Edie Reeder Adcock.

**Bonnie Bailey Adcock** (1907-1993) He was the son of John Franklin and Edie Reeder Adcock. He married Pauline E. Anthony.

**Pauline E. Anthony** (1909-1987) She was the wife of Bonnie Bailey "Bon" Adcock.

**A.F. "Alex" Spain** (1855-1936) He was the father of Cheat Spain Adcock.

**Martha Elam Spain** (1859-1942) Wife of Alex Spain and mother of Cheat Spain Adcock.

**Joseph Pyles** (1823-1907) He was the wife of Louisa Reeder Pyles and the father of James Thomas Pyles. James Thomas Pyles married Mary Ellen Adcock, daughter of Anderson and Caroline Smiley Adcock.

**Louisa J. Reeder** (1829-1896) She was the wife of Joseph Pyles. She was the daughter of Jonathan and Elizabeth Brumbelow Reeder.

**Cleva Jane Collier Adcock** (1899-1932) She married Adis Hugh Adcock. Adis was the son of John Franklin and Henrietta Reeder Adcock.

# Forest Grove Cemetery

**Directions:** From the intersection of Whites Creek Pike and I-24, go north on Whites Creek Pike about 2.9 miles. Turn left onto small road across from Forest Grove United Methodist Church. It is clearly marked. The cemetery is a few yards from Whites Creek Pike.

There are too many of our relations in Forest Grove Cemetery to list in this book. The cemetery, which began about 1870, is maintained by Forest Grove United Methodist Church. The church has a small congregation who shoulders the financial responsibility for the upkeep of this cemetery. Anyone wishing to make contributions to the church for their on-going efforts to keep this special place of rest clean and beautiful can send them to the Cemetery Fund, Forest Grove United Methodist Church, 7982 Whites Creek Pike, Joelton, TN 37080.

# From the Authors

"We are very blessed to have a long history of a family that handed down so much to us. We still hold to a lot of the traditions from one generation to the next. We walk where they walked and we swim and fish where they did. How great is that?"

*Carolyn Adcock-Smith – February 13, 2014*

" This is a real story about things that really happened. Overall, it's a positive story, full of ups and downs, with an on-going theme that life is good, life goes on, and we endure and never give up our quest for love, home and happiness."

*John R. Coles – August 10, 2017*

Made in the USA
Lexington, KY
10 May 2018